Reflections on Calvary's Cross

Joshua Rhoades

Published by Joshua Paul Rhoades, 2024.

While every precaution has been taken in the preparation of this book, the publisher assumes no responsibility for errors or omissions, or for damages resulting from the use of the information contained herein.

REFLECTIONS ON CALVARY'S CROSS

First edition. October 13, 2024.

Copyright © 2024 Joshua Rhoades.

ISBN: 979-8227601858

Written by Joshua Rhoades.

Also by Joshua Rhoades

Courage Under Fire: David's Stand On The Battlefield
Jonah's Journey: Voices Of Redemption And Lessons In Obedience
The Furnace Of Faith: 12 Principles From The Heat Of Faith
Whispers of Hope: Inspiring Stories of Men's Prayers In Scripture
Frontier Legends: The Oregon Dream
Elijah: A Beacon Of Boldness
HOOK, LINE & SAVIOUR - Faith Reflections from Fishing
Driven By Faith: Motor Racing Inspired Christian Life
30 Day Devotional - Bold and Strong- Coffee Devotions for a Courageous
Christian Walk
Authentic Christianity: The Heart of Old Time Religion
Consider The Ant - God's Tiny Preachers
Flee Fornication: The Plea For Purity
Renewed Hope- How to Find Encouragement in God
Sounding The Call - The Voice of Conviction
The Altar - Where Heaven Meets Earth
The Bible's Battlefields- Timeless Lessons from Ancient Wars
The Sacred Art of Silence - How Silence Speaks in Scripture
Under Fire- The Sanctity of the Traditional Biblical Home
Who Is on the Lord's Side? A Call to Righteousness
What Is Truth? - From Skepticism to Submission
First and Goal- Faith and Football Fundamentals
From Dugout to Devotion- Spiritual Lessons from Baseball
Par for the Course- Faith and Fairways
The Believer's Pace- Tools for Running Life's Marathon
The Immutable Fortress- Security in God's Unchanging Nature
Biblical Bravery
Deer Stands and Devotions: A Hunter's Walk with God

Jesus Knows- Our Hearts, Our Responsibility
Restoration - Setting The Bone
Spiritual 911- God's Word for Life's Emergency's
The Freedom of Forgiveness
The Jezebel Effect - Ancient Manipulations Modern Lessons
The Shout That Stopped The Saviour
The Time Machine Chronicles: Old Testament Characters
Anchored In Truth Exploring The Depths of Psalm 119
Biblical Counsel on Anger
Proverbs' Portraits The Men God Mentions
Stumbling in the Dark - The Dangers of Alcohol
Guarding the Wicket Protecting Your Faith and Game
The Champion's Faith - Wrestling and Achieving Spiritual Victory
Scriptural Commands for Modern Times Living God's Word Today Volume 1
Scriptural Commands for Modern Times Living God's Word Today Volume 2
Scriptural Commands for Modern Times Living God's Word TodayVolume3
The Greatest Gift
A Christmas Journey of Faith
Daughter Of The King: Embracing Your Identity In Christ
Determination and Dedication Building Strong Faith As A Young Man
Walking Through Walls God's Power to Part the Storms of Life
David's Song Of Deliverance Praising God Through Every Storm
From Weakness to Warrior: Gideon's Transformation
Why Did Jesus Weep?
Living For God The Call To Be A Living Sacrifice
My Mind Is In A Fog What Do I Do?
Turning The Page Written By Grace
The Calling and Greatness of John the Baptist
For Such a Time Esther's Courageous Stand
From Brokenness To Beauty Written By The Pen of Grace
The Ultimate Guide to Massive Action- From Plans to Reality
A Heart Of Conviction
Serving In The Shadows
Repentance Revealed The Road Back To God
The Chief Sinner Meets The Chief Saviour Reflections On I Timothy 1:15

Answer The Call - 31 Days of Biblical Action
The Birthmark of the Believer
Reflections on Calvary's Cross

Dedication

This book, "Reflections on Calvary's Cross," is dedicated to you, the reader, who may be searching for hope, peace, or a deeper understanding of God's love. No matter where you are in life—whether you're facing struggles, carrying heavy burdens, or feeling lost—this book is meant to remind you that there is always hope in the message of Calvary. The cross is where love, grace, and forgiveness meet, and it stands as a constant reminder that God's love for you is greater than anything you can imagine. Jesus' sacrifice on the cross wasn't just for the world in general; it was for you, personally. He saw your pain, your failures, and your fears, and He willingly gave His life to offer you redemption, peace, and a new beginning. As you read through these reflections, may you be encouraged to know that you are not alone. No matter how difficult life may seem, or how far you feel from God, His arms are always open to receive you, just as you are. The cross is a symbol of victory over sin, death, and darkness. It is a place where brokenness is healed, where guilt is erased, and where hope is restored. Jesus' sacrifice was not just a one-time event—it continues to impact your life today, offering you the strength, courage, and love you need to keep moving forward. If you feel weary, remember that Jesus invites you to come to Him, to lay your burdens at His feet, and to find rest in His love. His grace is enough for whatever you are going through. You don't have to carry the weight of your struggles alone—Jesus already carried them to the cross for you. The message of Calvary's Cross is that there is nothing too great for God's love to overcome. It is a love that is powerful enough to bring you through any trial, any loss, and any heartache. It is a love that meets you in your weakest moments and lifts you up with the promise of new life, renewed strength, and unshakable hope. As you reflect on the cross, let your heart be filled with the assurance that Jesus' sacrifice was for you, and that through His death and resurrection, you have been given the gift of eternal life and the promise of His presence every step of the way. This book is a reminder that Calvary's Cross is not just a symbol of suffering, but a beacon of hope and triumph. Whatever challenges you may face, know that you can face them with the knowledge that Jesus is with you, and His love is greater than anything that stands in your way. He has already won the victory, and that victory is yours. Let these reflections encourage you, strengthen your faith, and draw you closer to the One who loves you more than you could ever comprehend. You are cherished, you are redeemed, and you are never alone.

Introduction

"Reflections on Calvary's Cross" is a journey into the heart of the most important moment in history—the crucifixion of Jesus Christ. Calvary is not just a place in the past; it is the very center of the Christian faith, the place where love, sacrifice, and grace were fully displayed. As we reflect on the cross, we are drawn into the story of a Savior who gave everything for us, enduring unimaginable pain and suffering so that we could be forgiven and free. This book is not just about recounting the events of that day; it's about understanding the deep meaning behind it and how it changes everything for us. The cross is where the greatest act of love was shown, as Jesus willingly laid down His life for the sins of the world. It's where the penalty for sin was paid in full, once and for all, giving us hope and salvation. It is where, in His final moments, Jesus declared, "It is finished," proclaiming that the work of redemption was complete. As you read through these reflections, you will be reminded of the incredible sacrifice that was made at Calvary, not just for the world, but for you personally. This is a story of deep, sacrificial love, one that reminds us of how far God was willing to go to rescue us from the power of sin and death. Through the cross, Jesus not only conquered sin but also opened the door to eternal life, giving hope to the hopeless, peace to the troubled, and forgiveness to the broken. Each reflection in this book will take you deeper into the meaning of the cross, helping you understand its power, its significance, and how it calls each of us to respond with gratitude, faith, and a life transformed by grace. As you ponder the events of Calvary, may you find yourself drawn closer to the heart of Jesus, the one who suffered and died so that we might live. The cross is not just a symbol of suffering; it is a symbol of victory—a victory that was won for you. It is a place of both sorrow and joy, a place of pain and healing, a place where death was defeated, and life was given. The reflections in this book are meant to remind you that the cross is not just a historical event; it is the defining moment that offers hope to all who believe. It is a story that should never grow old, because it speaks to the deepest needs of the human heart—our need for love, forgiveness, and redemption. As you reflect on Calvary's cross, may you be reminded of the price that was paid for your freedom, and may your heart be filled with gratitude for the Savior who gave His all for you. This is not just a story about what happened long ago; it is a story that continues to impact our lives today, a story that invites us to live in the light of what was accomplished on that hill called Calvary. Let these reflections draw you nearer to the Savior who endured the cross, despising its shame, all because of His great love for you. May the cross of Christ always be at the center of your faith, your hope, and your life, and may these reflections help you see, with fresh eyes, the depth of the sacrifice made at Calvary. Through these pages, may you be reminded again and again of the overwhelming, never-ending love of God that was poured out for you on the cross, and may that love change you from the inside out. As you reflect on Calvary's cross, may you be moved to live a life that honors the One who gave His life for you.

Chapter 1 - Place of Sacrifice

Calvary is known as the place of sacrifice because it is where Jesus Christ offered Himself as the ultimate sacrifice for the sins of humanity. This single act of sacrifice, as described in Hebrews 9:26, changed the course of history forever. The word "sacrifice" means giving up something valuable for the sake of others, and that's exactly what Jesus did. He didn't just give up something small—He gave up His own life. Calvary, also known as Golgotha, is the place where Jesus was crucified, a place of pain, suffering, and death. But for Christians, it is much more than that; it is a place where love and forgiveness were demonstrated in the most powerful way. Jesus was the Son of God, completely without sin, but He took the punishment for our sins on Himself. The Bible tells us that all people have sinned and fallen short of the glory of God. Sin separates us from God because He is holy and perfect, and we are not. In the Old Testament, people would offer animal sacrifices as a way to atone for their sins. These sacrifices were a temporary solution, and they had to be repeated over and over again because they couldn't permanently take away sin. But when Jesus came, He came to be the final, perfect sacrifice that would take away sin once and for all. This is why Calvary is called the place of sacrifice. Jesus went to the cross willingly. He wasn't forced to go. He chose to die because He loved us so much. The sacrifice He made at Calvary was unlike any other. It was a one-time, all-sufficient sacrifice that covers the sins of everyone who believes in Him. The fact that Jesus, who was without sin, would take on the sins of the world is a remarkable act of love. The cross, which was a tool of punishment and death used by the Romans, became a symbol of hope and salvation because of what happened at Calvary. Jesus endured incredible physical suffering on the cross. He was beaten, mocked, and nailed to the cross where He hung for hours in agony. But the physical pain was not the only thing He suffered. He also bore the spiritual weight of all the sins of the world.

Imagine the emotional and spiritual pain of taking on the guilt, shame, and punishment for every wrong thing that has ever been done by every person throughout history. It's hard to fully comprehend the magnitude of what Jesus endured at Calvary. Yet, He did it because He loves us and wanted to make a way for us to be forgiven and have a relationship with God. The sacrifice at Calvary was the ultimate demonstration of love. Jesus Himself said, "Greater love has no one than this: to lay down one's life for one's friends." And that's exactly what He did at Calvary—He laid down His life for us, even though we didn't deserve it. He didn't die for perfect people; He died for sinners, for people who make mistakes, for people who sometimes choose their own way instead of God's way. And because of His sacrifice, those who believe in Him can be forgiven and have eternal life. The place of sacrifice, Calvary, reminds Christians of the seriousness of sin and the incredible love of God. Sin isn't something to be taken lightly. It's what separates us from God and leads to spiritual death. But because of what Jesus did at Calvary, the power of sin has been broken. When He died on the cross, He paid the price for our sins, and when He rose from the dead three days later, He showed that He had conquered death. This means that anyone who believes in Jesus can have eternal life, not because of anything they have done, but because of what Jesus did at Calvary. The cross at Calvary also shows us the depth of Jesus' obedience to God the Father. Jesus knew what was going to happen to Him, and He prayed in the Garden of Gethsemane before His arrest, asking if there was any other way to accomplish God's plan. But He ended His prayer by saying, "Not my will, but yours be done." Jesus was willing to follow God's plan, even though it meant going to the cross and enduring such pain and suffering. His obedience at Calvary is an example for Christians to follow. It shows that sometimes following God's plan isn't easy or comfortable, but it is always worth it. The place of sacrifice teaches us that true love is sacrificial. Jesus didn't just talk about love; He showed it by giving up His life for others. He didn't ask what was easiest or most comfortable for Him. He thought about what was best for us, and He gave everything. This kind of love is powerful, and it changes lives. When Christians look to the cross and remember the sacrifice that Jesus made at Calvary, they are reminded of the love that God has for them. It is a love that is unconditional, a love that doesn't depend on how good or bad we are, but simply on who God is. God is love, and Calvary is the place where that love was shown in the most powerful way. At Calvary, the place of sacrifice, Jesus took the punishment for sin so that we wouldn't have to. He experienced the separation from God that sin causes so that we could be brought close to God. His sacrifice made a way for people to be forgiven and have a relationship with God. And this forgiveness is available to everyone, no matter who they are or what they've done. It doesn't matter how many mistakes a person has made or how far they feel from God. Because of what Jesus did at Calvary, there is always hope, always a way to be forgiven and start fresh. The place of sacrifice is also a place of victory. When Jesus died on the cross, it might have seemed like defeat, but it was actually the greatest victory ever won. Jesus defeated sin, death, and Satan through His death and resurrection. The cross at Calvary is not a symbol of defeat but a symbol of victory. It is a reminder that no matter how dark things may seem, God has the final word, and His word is life, hope, and salvation. In conclusion, Calvary is the place of sacrifice where Jesus Christ offered Himself as the ultimate sacrifice for the sins of humanity. His death on the cross was a one-time, perfect sacrifice that provides forgiveness and eternal life to all who believe in Him. Calvary is a place of love, obedience, and victory. It is the place where Jesus' love for humanity was shown in the most powerful way, where sin was defeated, and where the door to eternal life was opened. For Christians, the cross at Calvary is the central symbol of their faith because it reminds them of the sacrifice that was made on their behalf and the love that God has for them. The sacrifice at Calvary was not just a historical event—it is something that continues to impact lives today, offering hope, forgiveness, and the promise of eternal life to all who believe.

Chapter 2 - Place of Fulfillment

Calvary, known as the place of fulfillment, holds a significant role in Christian belief because it is where the crucifixion of Jesus Christ occurred, fulfilling Old Testament prophecies about the Messiah's suffering and death. The Bible is full of prophecies, especially in the Old Testament, that spoke about a promised Savior, called the Messiah, who would come to save people from their sins. One of the most important prophecies about this Messiah can be found in Isaiah 53:5, which describes how the Messiah would be wounded for our transgressions, bruised for our iniquities, and how the punishment that brings us peace would be upon Him. This prophecy, written hundreds of years before Jesus was born, pointed to the fact that the Messiah would suffer in a very specific way. At Calvary, this prophecy was fulfilled in a way that no one could have expected.

The people of Israel were waiting for a Messiah, but many of them expected a king or a warrior who would free them from their political enemies, like the Romans, who were ruling over them at the time. They thought the Messiah would come with power and glory, leading an army to victory. But instead, Jesus came in humility. He was not born into a palace; He was born in a stable. He did not ride into Jerusalem on a mighty horse; He came on a donkey. And when it was time for Him to complete His mission, it was not by leading an army, but by dying on a cross. This is what makes Calvary the place of fulfillment. Jesus didn't fulfill the prophecies of a conquering king in the way people expected. Instead, He fulfilled the deeper, more important prophecies about a Savior who would suffer and die to save people from their sins.

The crucifixion at Calvary was the moment when all the pieces of God's plan came together. From the very beginning, when sin first entered the world through Adam and Eve, God had a plan to rescue humanity from the consequences of sin. That plan was to send His Son, Jesus, to live a perfect life and then to die as a sacrifice for the sins of the world. This plan is woven throughout the entire Bible, and Calvary is the place where it was fulfilled. The Old Testament is filled with prophecies that point to Jesus. Isaiah 53 is one of the clearest examples, but there are many others as well. For example, in Psalm 22, which was written by King David, there is a detailed description of the suffering that the Messiah would endure. It talks about how His hands and feet would be pierced, how people would mock Him, and how they would cast lots for His clothing. All of these things happened to Jesus during the crucifixion at Calvary. His hands and feet were pierced when He was nailed to the cross. The Roman soldiers mocked Him, calling Him the King of the Jews, and they cast lots to decide who would get to keep His clothes. These details might seem small, but they are incredibly important because they show that Jesus' death on the cross was not an accident. It was part of God's plan, a plan that had been foretold in Scripture long before it happened.

At Calvary, Jesus fulfilled not only the prophecies about His suffering but also the prophecies about how He would bring salvation to the world. In the Old Testament, God's people, the Israelites, had a system of sacrifices that they followed to atone for their sins. They would sacrifice animals like lambs, and the blood of these animals would be a temporary covering for their sins. But these sacrifices were never meant to be permanent. They were a symbol of something greater that was to come. The sacrifices pointed to Jesus, who would be the final and ultimate sacrifice. When Jesus died on the cross, He became the Lamb of God, the perfect and sinless sacrifice who took away the sins of the world once and for all. The sacrifices of the Old Testament had to be repeated over and over again because they could never fully take away sin. But Jesus' sacrifice at Calvary was different. It was perfect and complete, and it fulfilled the need for any further sacrifices. This is why Christians believe that Jesus' death on the cross is the only way to be saved from sin. He fulfilled the prophecies and the entire sacrificial system that had been set up in the Old Testament.

The fulfillment of these prophecies at Calvary shows us something very important about God: He keeps His promises. God had promised to send a Savior, and He did. Even though it didn't happen in the way people expected, it happened in exactly the way God had planned. This gives Christians confidence that they can trust God to keep His promises. If He fulfilled His promise to send a Savior, then they can trust Him to fulfill His other promises as well. Another important aspect of the fulfillment of prophecy at Calvary is that it shows the incredible love of God. The fact that Jesus would suffer and die for the sins of the world is the greatest act of love in history. Jesus didn't have to die. He could have chosen to save Himself. But He willingly went to the cross because of His love for humanity. He knew that the only way to bring people back into a relationship with God was to take the punishment for sin upon Himself. This is what the prophecies in Isaiah 53 and other parts of the Old Testament were pointing to—the love of a Savior who would take the place of sinners and suffer on their behalf.

The crucifixion at Calvary was also the fulfillment of the prophecy that the Messiah would bring peace. Isaiah 53:5 says that the punishment that brought us peace was upon Him. This means that through Jesus' death, the separation between God and humanity caused by sin was healed. Jesus took the punishment that we deserved so that we could have peace with God. This peace is not just a feeling of calm; it is a deep, spiritual peace that comes from knowing that our sins are forgiven and that we are in a right relationship with God. At Calvary, Jesus fulfilled the prophecy of bringing peace not just to the people of Israel, but to the whole world. His sacrifice was for all people, regardless of their background or nationality. This is why the message of the cross is for everyone. It is a message of hope, forgiveness, and peace that is available to all who believe in Jesus.

The fulfillment of prophecy at Calvary also shows that Jesus is the true King, but not in the way that people expected. Many people thought the Messiah would be a political leader who would overthrow the Roman government and restore Israel to its former glory. But Jesus' kingdom is not of this world. His reign is not about political power or military might. Instead, it is about love, sacrifice, and serving others. When Jesus was crucified, the Roman soldiers placed a sign above His head that said, "Jesus of Nazareth, King of the Jews." They meant it as a mockery, but it was actually a statement of truth. Jesus is the King, not just of the Jews, but of the entire world. His death on the cross was the ultimate act of kingship because it was through His sacrifice that He won the victory over sin and death.

Calvary, as the place of fulfillment, is also the place where the greatest victory in history was won. On the surface, it might have looked like a defeat.

Jesus was mocked, beaten, and crucified. His followers were scattered, and it seemed like all hope was lost. But three days after His death, Jesus rose from the dead, proving that He had conquered sin and death once and for all. His resurrection was the ultimate fulfillment of the prophecies about the Messiah. It showed that not even death could hold Him down. Because of His resurrection, Christians believe that they too will one day be raised to eternal life. The victory that Jesus won at Calvary is not just a personal victory; it is a victory for all who believe in Him.

In conclusion, Calvary is the place of fulfillment because it is where the crucifixion of Jesus Christ brought to completion all of the Old Testament prophecies about the Messiah's suffering and death. Isaiah 53:5 and many other prophecies foretold that the Messiah would suffer for the sins of the world, and at Calvary, Jesus did just that. He fulfilled the sacrificial system of the Old Testament, becoming the perfect and final sacrifice that takes away the sins of the world. His death on the cross brought peace between God and humanity, and His resurrection three days later proved that He had conquered sin and death. The fulfillment of these prophecies shows that God keeps His promises, and that Jesus is the true King and Savior of the world. Calvary stands as a reminder of God's incredible love and the victory that was won through Jesus' sacrifice.

Chapter 3 - Pinnacle of Love

Calvary is known as the pinnacle of love because it is the place where the greatest act of love in history took place. At Calvary, Jesus Christ willingly laid down His life for sinners, as described in John 15:13, which says, "Greater love hath no man than this, that a man lay down his life for his friends." What makes this act so powerful and unique is that Jesus didn't just die for His friends or for people who were good and deserving; He died for everyone, even for people who didn't love Him back, people who mocked Him, rejected Him, and even those who crucified Him. This is what makes Calvary the ultimate symbol of love, not just in the Bible but in all of human history. It was here that Jesus showed the world the depth of God's love, a love so deep and so strong that it led Him to sacrifice His own life to save others.

The love shown at Calvary wasn't a fleeting emotion or a temporary feeling. It was a deliberate choice. Jesus chose to die for the sins of the world, knowing full well what it would cost Him. He knew that He would have to endure incredible physical pain, emotional suffering, and spiritual separation from God the Father as He took on the sins of humanity. Yet, He did it willingly because of His immense love for people. This is the essence of true love—being willing to give everything for the sake of someone else, even if it means suffering and sacrifice.

Jesus' sacrifice at Calvary was not just a random act of kindness; it was a part of God's plan to save humanity from the consequences of sin. Sin is anything that separates people from God, and it's something that affects everyone. The Bible says that all have sinned and fallen short of the glory of God, and the penalty for sin is death—eternal separation from God. But because God loves people so much, He made a way for them to be saved. That way was through Jesus, who came to Earth, lived a perfect, sinless life, and then willingly gave up His life on the cross at Calvary to take the punishment for the sins of the world.

At Calvary, we see the greatest example of sacrificial love. Jesus didn't die because He had to; He died because He wanted to. He wanted to save humanity from the punishment of sin, and the only way to do that was to take on that punishment Himself. This act of love is hard to fully comprehend because it is so selfless and so profound. Most people would find it difficult to imagine giving up their life for someone else, especially for someone who had done nothing to deserve it. But that's exactly what Jesus did. He didn't just die for the people who loved Him or followed Him; He died for everyone, including those who rejected Him and turned away from Him. This is what makes Calvary the pinnacle of love—it was a love that reached out to all people, no matter who they were or what they had done.

One of the most remarkable things about the love shown at Calvary is that it was unconditional. Human love is often conditional. People tend to love those who are kind to them, who treat them well, or who do something for them. But the love that Jesus showed at Calvary was not based on conditions. It wasn't dependent on whether people deserved it or whether they would love Him in return. It was given freely, without strings attached. This kind of love is rare and almost impossible to find in the world today. It's a love that goes beyond what we can fully understand because it doesn't make sense by human standards. Yet, this is the love that Jesus demonstrated on the cross at Calvary.

The Bible tells us that while we were still sinners, Christ died for us. This means that Jesus didn't wait for people to clean up their lives or get everything right before He died for them. He died for people in their mess, in their brokenness, in their sin. He saw humanity at its worst, and He still loved them enough to give His life for them. This is the kind of love that can change lives. It's a love that reaches into the darkest places and brings light. It's a love that forgives, that heals, and that restores. And it all started at Calvary, the place where love reached its highest point.

The love of Jesus shown at Calvary was not just about physical suffering, although that was certainly part of it. Jesus endured incredible physical pain on the cross—He was beaten, whipped, and nailed to a wooden cross where He hung for hours in agony. But the physical pain was only part of the story. Jesus also experienced deep emotional and spiritual pain as He took on the sins of the world. In that moment, He felt the weight of every sin that had ever been committed and every sin that would ever be committed. He felt the separation from God that sin causes, something He had never experienced before. And yet, He endured it all because of His love for humanity.

At Calvary, Jesus showed that love is not just about words or feelings—it's about action. He didn't just say that He loved the world; He showed it by laying down His life. This is the ultimate example of love in action, and it's a powerful reminder that true love requires sacrifice. It's not always easy or comfortable, but it's always worth it. The love that Jesus demonstrated at Calvary continues to inspire people today, challenging them to love others in the same way—selflessly, sacrificially, and unconditionally.

Calvary also shows us that love has the power to conquer even the darkest and most difficult circumstances. The cross, which was a symbol of death, pain, and shame, was transformed into a symbol of hope, victory, and love because of what Jesus did. What seemed like the greatest defeat—Jesus' death—became the greatest victory, as He conquered sin and death through His resurrection. This shows that love is stronger than hate, stronger than sin, and even stronger than death. The love that was shown at Calvary didn't end with Jesus' death; it continues to this day, offering hope and salvation to all who believe in Him.

One of the most important things about the love shown at Calvary is that it's available to everyone. No one is excluded from this love. It doesn't matter who you are, where you come from, or what you've done—Jesus' love is for you. At Calvary, Jesus died for the sins of the whole world, offering forgiveness and new life to anyone who would accept it. This is why the cross is such a powerful symbol for Christians. It's a reminder that no matter how far someone has gone or how many mistakes they've made, they are never beyond the reach of God's love.

The love of Jesus shown at Calvary is also a love that brings freedom. Sin has a way of trapping people, making them feel guilty, ashamed, and separated from God. But Jesus' sacrifice at Calvary broke the power of sin and set people free. Through His death and resurrection, Jesus made it possible for people to be forgiven and to have a relationship with God. This is the greatest gift of love—freedom from sin and the promise of eternal life with God.

At Calvary, Jesus showed that love is not just a feeling; it's a choice. He chose to love humanity, even when it meant going to the cross. He chose to forgive, even when people didn't deserve it. He chose to give everything, even when it meant sacrificing His own life. This is the kind of love that changes everything. It's a love that goes beyond what is easy or convenient, a love that puts others first, and a love that is willing to give up everything for the sake of someone else.

In conclusion, Calvary represents the pinnacle of love because it is where Jesus Christ laid down His life for sinners. The love shown at Calvary was not just a feeling or an emotion—it was a deliberate, selfless act of sacrifice. Jesus willingly went to the cross, enduring incredible physical, emotional, and spiritual pain, because of His deep love for humanity. His love was unconditional, reaching out to everyone, regardless of whether they deserved it or not. It was a love that forgave, healed, and restored. It was a love that conquered sin, death, and darkness, transforming the cross from a symbol of defeat into a symbol of hope and victory. The love shown at Calvary continues to offer hope and salvation to all who believe, reminding us that no matter who we are or what we've done, we are never beyond the reach of God's love. Through His sacrifice at Calvary, Jesus showed the world what true love looks like—a love that is willing to give everything, even life itself, for the sake of others. This is why Calvary is the pinnacle of love, and why the love that was shown there will never be forgotten.

Chapter 4 - Price for Redemption

THE CONCEPT OF REDEMPTION is central to the Christian faith, and it revolves around one profound event—Jesus' death on the cross. This event is more than just a historical moment; it represents the price that was paid to redeem humanity from the bondage of sin. In the simplest terms, redemption means being bought back or rescued from a dire situation. For Christians, it means that Jesus Christ gave His life to pay the price for our freedom, freeing us from the power and consequences of sin. According to Ephesians 1:7, "In whom we have redemption through his blood, the forgiveness of sins, according to the riches of his grace." This verse clearly shows that Jesus' death on the cross was the cost that had to be paid to set humanity free. It was a price so great that no one else could pay it, and yet, Jesus paid it willingly out of His love for us.

To understand why Jesus had to die to redeem us, we need to start with the problem of sin. Sin is anything that goes against God's perfect will—actions, thoughts, or attitudes that are wrong in God's eyes. Ever since the first humans, Adam and Eve, disobeyed God in the Garden of Eden, sin has been a part of the human experience. Sin separates people from God, because God is holy and perfect, and sin cannot exist in His presence. The Bible tells us that "the wages of sin is death" (Romans 6:23). This means that the penalty for sin is not just physical death but eternal separation from God, which is spiritual death. It's a heavy consequence, but it's the natural result of sin because sin breaks our relationship with God.

In the Old Testament, God provided a system of sacrifices where people could offer animals like lambs or goats to atone for their sins. These sacrifices were a way for people to acknowledge their wrongdoing and seek forgiveness from God. However, these sacrifices were only temporary solutions. The blood of animals could not fully take away sin, and the sacrifices had to be repeated over and over again. They were symbolic of a greater sacrifice that was to come—the sacrifice of Jesus Christ. Jesus was the perfect, sinless Son of God, and He came to Earth with a specific mission: to pay the ultimate price for the sins of humanity through His death on the cross. This is why His death is often referred to as the "price for redemption."

When we talk about the price Jesus paid, we are talking about something far beyond money or material value. The price for redemption was His life. Jesus paid with His own blood, which is why the Bible often speaks of being redeemed by His blood. The cross was a brutal and painful way to die, but it was the means by which Jesus chose to save us. He was beaten, mocked, and nailed to a wooden cross, where He hung in agony for hours. But the physical pain was only part of the price He paid. Jesus also experienced the weight of the world's sins on His shoulders. Every lie, every act of hatred, every wrong thing that had ever been done or ever would be done—Jesus took all of it upon Himself. This is something that's hard to fully comprehend, but it shows just how deep His love is for us.

At the cross, Jesus took the punishment that we deserved. Sin requires justice, and the just penalty for sin is death. But instead of leaving us to face that punishment, Jesus stepped in and took it for us. He was our substitute. This is what makes His sacrifice so powerful and so life-changing. It wasn't just a random act of kindness; it was a deliberate choice to take on the punishment for sins He never committed so that we could be forgiven and set free. This is the heart of redemption. Jesus' death was not just about saving us from the penalty of sin; it was about breaking the power of sin in our lives. Before Jesus died, sin had a hold on humanity. It was like a chain that kept people bound, preventing them from living in true freedom. But through His death and resurrection, Jesus broke those chains. He paid the price to free us from the bondage of sin.

Redemption means that we are no longer slaves to sin. It means that we are no longer defined by our past mistakes, our failures, or our wrong choices. Jesus paid the price to give us a new identity—an identity as children of God. When we accept His sacrifice and believe in Him, we are forgiven, and our relationship with God is restored. This is the beauty of redemption: we are not only saved from something (sin and death), but we are also saved for something—a relationship with God and a life of purpose and freedom.

It's important to understand that redemption is not something we could have earned on our own. There is nothing we could do to pay the price for our own sins because the cost is too great. The Bible says that all our righteous acts are like filthy rags in comparison to God's holiness. No number of good deeds or effort could make up for the wrong we've done. This is why Jesus' death is such a gift. It's a gift of grace, which means it's something we don't deserve but is given to us out of God's love and kindness. Redemption is not about what we do; it's about what Jesus did for us.

The price for redemption was costly, but Jesus paid it willingly. He wasn't forced to go to the cross. In fact, at any moment, He could have chosen to walk away from His mission. But He didn't. In the Garden of Gethsemane, the night before His crucifixion, Jesus prayed to God, asking if there was any other way to accomplish His mission. But He ended His prayer with these words: "Not my will, but yours be done." Jesus knew the full weight of what was coming, and yet He chose to go through with it because He loved us. His willingness to lay down His life for us is the ultimate expression of love and the ultimate fulfillment of God's plan for redemption.

Redemption is not just about being saved from something bad; it's about being saved for something good. Through Jesus' death, we are not only forgiven, but we are also given new life. The Bible says that if anyone is in Christ, they are a new creation. The old has gone, and the new has come. This means that through Jesus' sacrifice, we are given a fresh start. Our sins are forgiven, our past is wiped clean, and we are free to live in the fullness of God's love and grace. This new life is not just about following rules or trying to be a good person; it's about being in a relationship with God, knowing that we are loved, forgiven, and redeemed.

One of the most amazing things about redemption is that it is available to everyone. No one is too far gone or too sinful to be redeemed. Jesus paid the price for all of humanity, not just for a select few. His death on the cross was for everyone—young and old, rich and poor, those who have made terrible mistakes and those who feel like they've lived a relatively good life. Redemption is a gift that is offered to all who believe in Jesus and accept His sacrifice.

It doesn't matter what you've done in your past or how far you feel from God—Jesus paid the price to bring you back into a relationship with Him.

Another important aspect of redemption is that it is complete. When Jesus died on the cross, He said, "It is finished." These were some of His final words before He took His last breath. What He meant by this was that the work of redemption was done. The price had been paid in full. There was nothing more that needed to be done to secure our salvation. Jesus' sacrifice was enough. This is why Christians believe that salvation is not based on what we do, but on what Jesus has already done. We don't have to earn our way to God; Jesus has already made the way for us through His death on the cross.

The redemption that Jesus offers is not just about the here and now; it's about eternity. Because of Jesus' death and resurrection, Christians believe that they will have eternal life with God. This is the ultimate result of redemption—eternal life free from the pain, suffering, and brokenness of this world. The Bible promises that for those who believe in Jesus, there is a future where there will be no more death, no more sorrow, and no more pain. This is the hope of redemption—the hope that one day, all things will be made new, and we will live forever in the presence of God.

In conclusion, Jesus' death on the cross was the price paid for our redemption. It was a price that no one else could pay, and yet Jesus paid it willingly because of His great love for us. Through His sacrifice, we are forgiven, set free from the bondage of sin, and given new life. Redemption is not something we could earn on our own; it is a gift of grace, offered to all who believe in Jesus. The price for our redemption was costly, but Jesus paid it in full, saying, "It is finished." Because of His death and resurrection, we have the hope of eternal life and the promise of a restored relationship with God. Redemption is not just about being saved from sin; it's about being saved for a life of freedom, purpose, and love in Christ. This is the incredible truth of the cross: that Jesus paid the ultimate price to set us free, and through Him, we are redeemed.

Chapter 5 - Place of Substitution

The idea of substitution is one of the most powerful concepts in the Christian faith, and it all centers around what Jesus did for us at the cross. The Bible tells us in 2 Corinthians 5:21, "For He hath made Him to be sin for us, who knew no sin; that we might be made the righteousness of God in Him." This verse sums up the incredible act of substitution that took place at Calvary. Jesus, who had never sinned, became the substitute for all of humanity. He took upon Himself the punishment that we deserved because of our sins, and in doing so, He gave us the opportunity to be made right with God. This is what makes Calvary such a significant and holy place—it's where the greatest act of love and sacrifice happened, where Jesus chose to stand in our place and take the penalty that was meant for us.

To understand the importance of substitution, we first need to understand the problem of sin. Sin is anything that goes against God's perfect and holy nature. It includes our wrong actions, harmful words, and even the selfish thoughts we have. From the moment Adam and Eve disobeyed God in the Garden of Eden, sin entered the world and has been a part of human life ever since. Sin separates us from God because God is holy and cannot be in the presence of sin. The Bible says that the wages of sin is death (Romans 6:23), meaning that the punishment for sin is not just physical death but eternal separation from God. This is a serious consequence, and it's something that affects every single person because we all sin. No matter how hard we try to be good, we all fall short of God's perfect standard.

This is where Jesus comes in as our substitute. In the Old Testament, people had a system of sacrifices where they would offer animals like lambs and goats to atone for their sins. These animals were meant to be a substitute for the person's sins—the animal would die in place of the person. But these sacrifices were temporary and had to be repeated over and over again because they could never fully take away sin. They were a symbol of the ultimate sacrifice that was to come—the sacrifice of Jesus Christ, who would be the final and perfect substitute for all of humanity's sins. When Jesus came to Earth, He lived a completely sinless life. He never sinned, not even once, which made Him the only one who could take the place of sinners and pay the price for their sins.

At the cross, a great exchange took place. Jesus, who had no sin, took on all of our sins. He took the guilt, shame, and punishment that we deserved. Imagine standing in a courtroom, knowing you are guilty of breaking the law and that the punishment is severe. Then, someone steps forward and says, "I will take the punishment for them. Let them go free, and I will pay the price." That is what Jesus did for us. He took our place, He took our punishment, and He bore the full weight of God's wrath against sin so that we wouldn't have to. He became the substitute for all of humanity, enduring the pain and suffering that was meant for us.

This act of substitution is the ultimate display of love. Jesus didn't have to do it. He could have stayed in heaven, away from the pain and suffering of this world. But He chose to come down, live among us, and ultimately die for us because of His great love for humanity. He knew that we could never save ourselves from the consequences of sin, so He took it upon Himself to be our Savior. This is why Christians believe that Jesus is the only way to be saved. His sacrifice on the cross was a one-time, perfect act of substitution that can never be repeated or replaced. There is nothing we can do on our own to earn salvation; it is a gift that Jesus offers to us because He took our place.

The pain and suffering that Jesus endured as our substitute were unimaginable. The physical agony of being nailed to a cross and left to hang for hours was excruciating. But the spiritual suffering was even greater. As Jesus hung on the cross, He experienced separation from God the Father for the first time in His existence. He cried out, "My God, my God, why have you forsaken me?" (Matthew 27:46). In that moment, Jesus took upon Himself the full weight of the world's sin. He experienced the separation from God that sin causes, and He did it so that we would never have to experience that separation ourselves. Jesus' suffering was not just physical; it was spiritual and emotional, and it was all done out of love for us.

One of the most remarkable things about Jesus' substitutionary sacrifice is that it was for everyone. Jesus didn't just die for a select group of people or for those who were "good enough." He died for all of humanity, for every single person who has ever lived or will ever live. This includes the people who mocked Him, the people who rejected Him, and even the people who nailed Him to the cross. His love is so vast and so deep that He was willing to die for even those who didn't love Him back. This is the heart of the gospel message—that Jesus died for sinners, and that includes every one of us. No matter who you are or what you've done, Jesus took your place on the cross.

Jesus' substitutionary death also means that we can be forgiven. Because Jesus took the punishment for our sins, we no longer have to bear that punishment ourselves. When we accept Jesus as our Savior, His sacrifice covers our sins, and we are forgiven. It's like having a debt that you could never repay, and someone steps in and pays it off for you. That's what Jesus did for us—He paid the debt of sin that we could never pay. And because of His sacrifice, we are no longer condemned by our sins. We are free, forgiven, and made right with God.

This is why Christians talk so much about grace. Grace is the idea that we are given something we don't deserve, and that's exactly what Jesus' substitutionary death on the cross is—it's a gift of grace. We didn't deserve for Jesus to take our place. We didn't deserve for Him to bear the punishment for our sins. But He did it anyway because of His love and grace. And this grace is available to everyone. No matter how far you've strayed, no matter how many mistakes you've made, Jesus' sacrifice covers it all. His death on the cross was sufficient to pay for the sins of the entire world.

When we accept Jesus as our substitute, something incredible happens. The Bible tells us that we are made new. We are no longer defined by our past mistakes or sins. Instead, we are given a new identity as children of God. This is part of the great exchange that took place at the cross—Jesus took on our sin, and in return, we are given His righteousness. This doesn't mean that we are suddenly perfect or that we never sin again, but it does mean that when God looks at us, He no longer sees our sins. He sees the righteousness of Jesus. This is what it means to be justified, to be made right with God. It's not because of anything we've done, but because of what Jesus did for us as our substitute.

The substitution of Jesus also brings hope. Before Jesus' death, sin and death had the final say. Sin led to death, and there was no way to escape it. But because Jesus took our place and conquered sin and death through His resurrection, we now have hope for the future. Death is no longer the end for those who believe in Jesus. Just as Jesus was raised from the dead, we too will be raised to eternal life with God. This is the hope of the resurrection, and it's all made possible because of what Jesus did as our substitute.

In conclusion, Jesus became the substitute for us, taking the punishment we deserved upon Himself at the cross. His death was not just an act of sacrifice; it was the ultimate act of love and grace. Jesus took our place, bore our sins, and paid the penalty that we could never pay. Through His substitutionary death, we are forgiven, set free from the power of sin, and given new life in Him. This is the heart of the Christian message—that Jesus died for sinners, and that includes every single one of us. His sacrifice was for everyone, and it offers us the gift of grace, forgiveness, and eternal life. The cross is where the greatest exchange took place—Jesus took our sins, and in return, we receive His righteousness. This is the incredible truth of the gospel, and it's what makes Jesus' death on the cross the most important event in history. As our substitute, Jesus made a way for us to be reconciled with God, to be made new, and to have the hope of eternal life. This is the message of the cross: Jesus took our place, and because of His love, we are saved.

Chapter 6 - Proof of God's Justice

At the heart of the Christian faith, Calvary stands as one of the most important moments in all of history. It was at Calvary, where Jesus Christ was crucified, that God's justice was fully satisfied. This concept can be difficult to understand, but it's at the core of why Christians believe in salvation through Jesus. The Bible tells us in Romans 3:25-26 that God presented Christ as a sacrifice of atonement, through the shedding of His blood, to demonstrate His righteousness. In simpler terms, this means that God showed He is just by punishing sin, but He did it in a way that allows us to be saved. Jesus bore the penalty for sin in our place. What makes this event so powerful is the combination of justice and mercy that took place at Calvary. God is perfectly just, which means that He cannot allow sin to go unpunished. At the same time, God is also merciful and loves humanity deeply. He didn't want us to be separated from Him forever because of our sins. The solution? Jesus Christ took the punishment that we deserved. This act of substitution satisfied God's justice while also making a way for us to be forgiven.

Understanding God's justice is key to grasping why Jesus' death at Calvary was necessary. From the beginning of the Bible, we see that sin has consequences. In the Garden of Eden, when Adam and Eve disobeyed God, they introduced sin into the world. This disobedience brought death, suffering, and separation from God into human existence. Every person since then has been born into a world marked by sin. And because God is holy, He cannot ignore or overlook sin. In human terms, it's like how a fair judge cannot simply let a criminal go free without any consequences. If God were to ignore sin, He would not be just. Sin must be dealt with, and the Bible says the penalty for sin is death (Romans 6:23). This death is not just physical but spiritual—eternal separation from God. Justice requires that the debt of sin be paid, and because all humans are sinful, we are all deserving of that punishment.

However, God, in His love and mercy, didn't want to leave us in that hopeless state. This is where the proof of God's justice at Calvary comes into play. God's plan was to send His Son, Jesus, to live a perfect life without sin and then to take upon Himself the punishment that we deserve. Jesus became the sacrificial lamb, offering Himself willingly to die in our place. In doing so, He took the weight of all our sins upon Himself, enduring the wrath of God so that we wouldn't have to. This act is called substitutionary atonement, meaning Jesus was our substitute, and His death made amends for our sins. At Calvary, God's justice was not compromised—sin was punished, but instead of us bearing the penalty, Jesus bore it for us. This is what makes the cross so incredible. It was the moment when God's justice and mercy met in perfect harmony.

It's important to recognize that Jesus didn't just suffer physical pain on the cross, though that alone was horrific. Crucifixion was one of the most brutal forms of execution in the ancient world, designed to cause maximum pain and humiliation. Jesus was beaten, mocked, and nailed to a cross where He hung in agony for hours. But even more than the physical pain, Jesus experienced the spiritual agony of bearing the sins of the world. For the first time in all eternity, Jesus was separated from God the Father as He took on the full punishment for sin. This separation was the true weight of the cross. When Jesus cried out, "My God, my God, why have you forsaken me?" (Matthew 27:46), it was because He was experiencing the spiritual death that sin brings—separation from God. This was the justice of God being carried out. Jesus took the punishment that was meant for us, so we could be spared.

In that moment, God's justice was fully satisfied. Every sin, no matter how small or great, was accounted for and paid in full by Jesus. This includes the sins of the past, present, and future. The cross of Calvary was a one-time event, but its impact stretches across all of time. Because of Jesus' sacrifice, God can now justly forgive sinners. He didn't just sweep sin under the rug or pretend it didn't happen. Instead, He dealt with it head-on by sending His Son to take the penalty. This is what makes God's justice so perfect—He doesn't ignore sin, but He also provides a way for us to be forgiven and reconciled to Him. Without the cross, we would still be under the judgment of sin, facing eternal separation from God. But because of Jesus, we have the opportunity to be made right with God.

The concept of justice being satisfied through Jesus' death is also a reminder of the seriousness of sin. Sin isn't just a minor mistake or a slip-up. It's a violation of God's holy law and a rejection of His perfect will. The fact that it took the death of God's own Son to atone for sin shows just how serious it is. Sin is destructive, and it separates us from the very source of life—God. When we look at the cross, we see not only the love of God but also the weight of our sin and the cost of our redemption. Jesus paid a price that we could never pay ourselves. This is why the Bible says we are "bought with a price" (1 Corinthians 6:20). That price was Jesus' own life, given freely so that we could be saved.

Another important aspect of God's justice being satisfied at Calvary is the fact that Jesus' sacrifice was voluntary. Jesus wasn't forced to go to the cross. In fact, at any moment, He could have stopped it. He could have called down legions of angels to rescue Him. But He didn't. Instead, He chose to endure the cross because of His love for us and His desire to fulfill God's plan of salvation. This makes His sacrifice even more meaningful. It wasn't just a tragic event or a random act of violence—it was part of God's plan from the very beginning. Jesus willingly took our place, knowing full well what it would cost Him. His love for humanity was so great that He was willing to suffer and die so that we could be saved. This is the ultimate proof of God's justice and mercy working together.

Because of what Jesus did at Calvary, we now have the opportunity to be forgiven and restored to a right relationship with God. When we accept Jesus as our Savior and believe in His sacrifice on the cross, God forgives our sins and declares us righteous in His sight. This is called justification, and it's a legal term that means we are declared not guilty. God no longer sees us as sinners deserving of punishment; instead, He sees us as righteous because of what Jesus did. This is the result of God's justice being satisfied. Sin has been punished, and we are now free from the penalty of death. This is why Christians talk so much about grace—because salvation is not something we could ever earn or deserve. It's a gift from God, made possible by Jesus' sacrifice at Calvary.

The proof of God's justice at Calvary also gives us hope for the future. Because sin has been dealt with, we can look forward to eternal life with God. Jesus' death and resurrection were not the end of the story—they were the beginning of a new chapter for humanity. Through His resurrection, Jesus conquered death, and because of that, we have the hope of eternal life. God's justice ensures that evil will not have the final say. One day, all sin and death will be completely wiped away, and those who have put their trust in Jesus will live with God forever in a world that is free from sin, suffering, and death. This is the ultimate fulfillment of God's justice and love.

In conclusion, Calvary is the place where God's justice was satisfied. Jesus took upon Himself the punishment that we deserved for our sins. His death on the cross was the ultimate act of substitution, and it demonstrated both the seriousness of sin and the depth of God's love. By bearing the penalty for sin in our place, Jesus made a way for us to be forgiven and reconciled to God. At Calvary, God's justice and mercy met in a perfect display of love. Sin was not ignored, but it was fully dealt with through the sacrifice of Jesus. This is the heart of the Christian message—that through Jesus, we can be forgiven, justified, and given the hope of eternal life. The cross is the proof that God's justice is real, but so is His incredible love for humanity. It is the place where the greatest act of love and the most profound act of justice came together, changing the course of history and offering salvation to all who believe.

Chapter 7 - Power of Forgiveness

The power of forgiveness is one of the most incredible and life-changing truths in the Christian faith, and it all comes from what happened at Calvary. At Calvary, Jesus Christ shed His blood on the cross, and through that sacrifice, humanity is offered forgiveness and the chance to be reconciled with God. In Colossians 1:14, it says, "In whom we have redemption through his blood, even the forgiveness of sins." This verse sums up the amazing gift that Jesus gave to the world. His death on the cross wasn't just a sad moment in history—it was the moment when everything changed. Through His blood, Jesus made it possible for all of humanity to be forgiven of their sins and to have a restored relationship with God. This forgiveness is more than just letting go of mistakes or saying, "I'm sorry." It is a complete erasure of guilt, shame, and the punishment we deserve for our sins. The power of forgiveness that came from Calvary is what sets people free and gives them new life, and it is available to everyone who believes in Jesus.

To understand why this forgiveness is so powerful, we need to first understand what sin is and how it affects our relationship with God. Sin is anything that goes against God's perfect will. It includes our actions, thoughts, and attitudes that are selfish, harmful, and contrary to what God desires for us. Every person has sinned, and because of that, we are all separated from God. Sin creates a barrier between us and God, and no matter how hard we try, we can't break that barrier on our own. The Bible says that the wages of sin is death (Romans 6:23), meaning that the consequence of sin is not just physical death, but eternal separation from God. It's a serious problem because God is holy and perfect, and sin cannot exist in His presence. This separation from God is what makes people feel empty, lost, and disconnected. We were created to have a relationship with God, but sin breaks that connection.

However, God didn't want to leave us in this broken state. That's where the power of forgiveness comes in. God, in His love and mercy, made a way for us to be forgiven and reconciled to Him. He sent His Son, Jesus, to die on the cross and take the punishment for our sins. Jesus lived a perfect, sinless life, and He didn't deserve to die, but He willingly laid down His life so that we could be forgiven. The blood that Jesus shed on the cross was the payment for our sins. In the Old Testament, people would offer sacrifices of animals to atone for their sins. These sacrifices were a temporary way for people to seek forgiveness, but they had to be repeated over and over again because they couldn't fully take away sin. But when Jesus died on the cross, He became the ultimate and final sacrifice. His blood was shed once for all, and it was powerful enough to forgive every sin—past, present, and future.

The forgiveness that comes through Jesus' blood is complete. It doesn't just cover up our sins or push them to the side—it removes them entirely. The Bible says that when God forgives us, He remembers our sins no more (Hebrews 8:12). This means that once we are forgiven, our sins are completely wiped away. It's like having a debt that you could never repay, and someone steps in and pays it off for you. That's what Jesus did on the cross. He paid the debt of sin that we owed, and because of that, we are no longer held guilty for our sins. This is what makes forgiveness so powerful—it sets us free from the weight of guilt and shame. Many people carry around the burden of their past mistakes, feeling like they are defined by what they've done wrong. But through Jesus' sacrifice, that burden is lifted. We are no longer defined by our sins; we are defined by God's love and grace.

Forgiveness also brings reconciliation with God. Before we are forgiven, we are separated from God because of our sin. But through Jesus, that separation is healed. The relationship that was broken by sin is restored. This is what reconciliation means—being brought back into a right relationship with God. When we are forgiven, we are no longer distant from God; we are His children. We can come to Him with confidence, knowing that He loves us and accepts us. This restored relationship with God is one of the most beautiful aspects of forgiveness. It means that we are no longer cut off from the source of life, hope, and peace. Instead, we are connected to God, who gives us everything we need to live a full and meaningful life.

One of the amazing things about the forgiveness that comes through Jesus is that it is available to everyone. No matter who you are, where you come from, or what you've done, you can be forgiven. There is no sin too great for God to forgive. Sometimes people feel like they've made too many mistakes or gone too far for God to forgive them. But the Bible makes it clear that Jesus' sacrifice was enough to cover every sin. When He died on the cross, He said, "It is finished" (John 19:30), meaning that the work of forgiveness was complete. There is nothing more that needs to be done because Jesus' blood was powerful enough to forgive all sin. This is why the message of the cross is such good news—it offers hope and forgiveness to everyone, no matter how broken or lost they feel.

Forgiveness also brings freedom. Sin has a way of trapping people, making them feel stuck in patterns of guilt, shame, and failure. But when we are forgiven, we are set free from the power of sin. We no longer have to be controlled by our past mistakes or live in fear of punishment. Jesus' death on the cross broke the chains of sin and set us free to live in the fullness of God's grace. This doesn't mean that we will never struggle or make mistakes again, but it does mean that we are no longer slaves to sin. We are free to live the life that God created us to live—a life of love, joy, and peace. This is the power of forgiveness: it not only cleanses us from our sins, but it also empowers us to live differently.

Another important aspect of forgiveness is that it brings healing. Sin doesn't just damage our relationship with God; it also damages our relationships with others and even with ourselves. When we are caught in sin, it often leads to hurt, brokenness, and pain. But forgiveness brings healing to those wounds. When we are forgiven by God, it allows us to forgive ourselves and others. Jesus taught His followers to forgive others just as they have been forgiven (Matthew 6:14-15). This is because forgiveness is not just something we receive; it's something we are called to give. When we experience the power of God's forgiveness in our own lives, it gives us the strength to forgive those who have hurt us. This kind of forgiveness can bring healing to broken relationships and restore peace where there has been conflict. It also brings inner healing, freeing us from the bitterness and anger that often come with unforgiveness.

Forgiveness also brings peace. When we are forgiven, we are no longer at odds with God. We are at peace with Him, knowing that our sins have been forgiven and that we are accepted by Him. This peace is not just a feeling; it's a deep sense of security that comes from knowing that we are right with God. It's the peace that comes from knowing that we are loved, forgiven, and secure in our relationship with Him. This peace can carry us through the challenges of life, giving us the strength to face difficulties with confidence, knowing that God is with us and for us.

The power of forgiveness through Jesus' blood also gives us hope. Before we are forgiven, sin leaves us feeling hopeless and separated from God. But through Jesus, we have the hope of eternal life. Jesus' death and resurrection opened the way for us to be with God forever. This is the ultimate hope of forgiveness—that one day, we will be with God in a place where there is no more sin, no more suffering, and no more death. This hope gives meaning to our lives now and gives us the strength to endure difficult times, knowing that there is something greater waiting for us in the future.

In conclusion, the power of forgiveness is one of the greatest gifts that Jesus gave to humanity through His death on the cross at Calvary. Through His blood, we are offered complete forgiveness of our sins and reconciliation with God. This forgiveness sets us free from the guilt and shame of our past mistakes, restores our relationship with God, and gives us the hope of eternal life. It is a gift that is available to everyone, no matter who they are or what they've done. The power of forgiveness not only cleanses us from sin but also brings healing, peace, and freedom. It is a life-changing gift that allows us to live in the fullness of God's love and grace. This is the incredible power of forgiveness that was made possible through the blood of Jesus at Calvary. It is the reason why Christians celebrate the cross, not as a symbol of death, but as a symbol of life, hope, and redemption.

Chapter 8 - Pardon for Sinners

Calvary is one of the most powerful symbols in the Christian faith, known as the place, where Jesus Christ offered His life as a sacrifice to bring pardon for sinners. This pardon is not just for a select few; it is for all who repent of their sins and believe in Him. The idea of pardon means being forgiven, having the slate wiped clean, and being released from the guilt and punishment that sin brings. In Luke 23:34, as Jesus hung on the cross, He said, "Father, forgive them, for they know not what they do." These words capture the very heart of Jesus' mission at Calvary – to offer forgiveness and pardon even to those who were responsible for His suffering and death. This moment represents the incredible depth of God's love for humanity, a love so profound that it moved Him to provide a way for sinners to be reconciled to Him through the death of His Son.

To understand why this pardon is so significant, we first need to grasp the seriousness of sin. Sin is anything that goes against God's will and character. It includes our wrong actions, harmful words, selfish thoughts, and even the things we fail to do that we should. Every person has sinned, and because of that, we are all separated from God. Sin creates a barrier between humanity and God, and it leads to spiritual death, which means eternal separation from God. This separation is the most tragic consequence of sin because God created us to be in a relationship with Him, but sin breaks that connection. Sin is not just a minor issue; it is a serious problem that affects every part of our lives and our world. It leads to broken relationships, pain, suffering, and ultimately, death. The Bible makes it clear that the wages of sin is death (Romans 6:23), and this death is both physical and spiritual. Spiritual death means being cut off from God, the source of life and goodness.

However, God, in His great love for us, did not want to leave us in this hopeless state. He had a plan to rescue us, a plan that was centered on Jesus

Christ and His sacrifice at Calvary. Jesus came to Earth not just to teach and heal, but to lay down His life as a ransom for many (Matthew 20:28). His death on the cross was the fulfillment of God's plan to provide pardon for sinners. At Calvary, Jesus took upon Himself the punishment that we deserved for our sins. He, who was sinless and perfect, became the substitute for all of humanity. His death was not just an ordinary death – it was a sacrificial death, a death that had the power to forgive sins and restore the broken relationship between God and people. Jesus' willingness to endure the suffering and humiliation of the cross shows the extent of His love for us. He was willing to pay the ultimate price so that we could be pardoned and set free from the consequences of sin.

Pardon for sinners means that those who repent and believe in Jesus are forgiven of their sins. Repentance is not just feeling sorry for what we've done wrong; it is a complete turning away from sin and turning toward God. It is acknowledging that we have sinned and asking God for forgiveness. Belief in Jesus means trusting in Him as our Savior, the one who paid the price for our sins on the cross. When we repent and believe in Jesus, we receive the gift of pardon, which means that God forgives us completely. He no longer holds our sins against us, and we are no longer under the judgment of sin. This pardon is a gift of grace, meaning that it is not something we can earn or deserve. It is given to us freely because of God's great love and mercy.

The pardon that Jesus offers is complete and final. When He died on the cross, He took upon Himself all of our sins – past, present, and future. His sacrifice was enough to cover every sin that has ever been committed or will ever be committed. This means that no matter how great or small our sins are, they can all be forgiven through Jesus' death. There is no sin too big for God's grace. Sometimes people feel like they have done too many wrong things or that their sins are too serious to be forgiven, but the Bible makes it clear that Jesus' sacrifice is powerful enough to forgive even the worst of sins. The moment we repent and believe in Jesus, we are completely pardoned, and our sins are washed away. We are made clean and given a fresh start.

One of the most amazing things about the pardon that comes from Calvary is that it is available to everyone. Jesus' death on the cross was for all people, not just for a select group. It doesn't matter who you are, where you come from, or what you've done – the offer of pardon is extended to you. Jesus' words on the cross, "Father, forgive them," were not just for the people who were physically present at His crucifixion; they were for all of humanity. His sacrifice was for the entire world, and His forgiveness is available to anyone who repents and believes. This is what makes the message of the cross such good news – it is a message of hope and redemption for all people. No one is beyond the reach of God's grace.

Pardon for sinners also means that we are set free from the guilt and shame of our sins. Sin has a way of weighing us down, making us feel unworthy and distant from God. But when we are pardoned, that weight is lifted. We no longer have to carry the burden of guilt because Jesus has taken it upon Himself. He bore the punishment for our sins so that we could be free from guilt and shame. This is one of the most freeing and life-changing aspects of pardon – it allows us to live in the freedom of God's grace. We are no longer defined by our past mistakes or failures; we are defined by God's love and forgiveness. When God pardons us, He no longer sees us as sinners; He sees us as His beloved children, forgiven and redeemed.

This pardon also brings reconciliation with God. Sin separates us from God, but through Jesus' sacrifice, that separation is healed. We are brought back into a right relationship with God, where we can know Him, love Him, and experience His presence in our lives. This is the ultimate goal of pardon – not just to forgive us of our sins, but to restore the relationship that was broken by sin. God created us to be in a relationship with Him, and through Jesus, that relationship is restored. This reconciliation brings peace, joy, and fulfillment because we are no longer distant from the One who created us and loves us more than we can imagine.

Another important aspect of the pardon that comes from Calvary is that it brings eternal life. The Bible tells us that the wages of sin is death, but the gift of God is eternal life through Jesus Christ our Lord (Romans 6:23). Because of Jesus' death on the cross, we are not only forgiven of our sins, but we are also given the promise of eternal life with God. This means that death is not the end for those who have been pardoned by Jesus. Instead, we have the hope of living forever with God in a place where there is no more sin, no more pain, and no more death. This is the ultimate result of the pardon that Jesus offers – not only are we forgiven, but we are also given the gift of eternal life.

In conclusion, Calvary is the place where Jesus' sacrifice brought pardon for all who repent and believe in Him. His death on the cross was the ultimate act of love and mercy, offering forgiveness to all who turn to Him in faith. Through His sacrifice, we are set free from the guilt and punishment of sin, reconciled to God, and given the promise of eternal life. This pardon is available to everyone, no matter who you are or what you've done. It is a gift of grace, given freely because of God's great love for humanity. When we repent and believe in Jesus, we are completely forgiven, our sins are washed away, and we are brought into a new and restored relationship with God. The pardon that comes from Calvary is life-changing, offering hope, freedom, and the promise of eternal life. It is the greatest gift that anyone could ever receive, and it is available to all who will turn to Jesus and accept it. This is the power of the cross – the place where Jesus' sacrifice brought pardon for sinners and opened the way for all to be reconciled to God.

Chapter 9 - Prophetic Significance

The crucifixion of Jesus at Calvary is one of the most significant events in all of history, not just because of what it achieved for humanity, but also because it was foretold long before it happened. The prophetic significance of the crucifixion is profound, showing how it was part of God's grand plan for salvation from the very beginning. The Bible is filled with prophecies that point to the coming of a Savior, and one of the clearest examples is found in Psalm 22:16, where it says, "For dogs have compassed me: the assembly of the wicked have enclosed me: they pierced my hands and my feet." This verse, written hundreds of years before Jesus was born, describes the very method of His death—crucifixion, where His hands and feet were pierced with nails. This prophecy and many others demonstrate that the crucifixion was not a random event. It was part of God's plan to save humanity from the very beginning, and it was fulfilled perfectly in Jesus' death on the cross.

To fully appreciate the prophetic significance of Calvary, it's important to understand how deeply the Old Testament is connected to the New Testament. Throughout the Old Testament, God revealed glimpses of His salvation plan through the words of prophets, kings, and even poets like David, who wrote Psalm 22. These prophecies pointed to a coming Messiah, a Savior who would rescue God's people from sin and restore their relationship with Him. The people of Israel longed for this Messiah, but many of them misunderstood what His mission would be. They expected a political leader or a warrior who would free them from their earthly enemies, but God's plan was much bigger than that. The salvation God was offering wasn't just about political freedom—it was about freedom from sin, death, and separation from Him. The crucifixion of Jesus was the fulfillment of this salvation plan, and it was foretold with incredible accuracy in the Scriptures.

Psalm 22 is one of the clearest examples of this prophetic foreshadowing. Written by King David, this psalm vividly describes the suffering of someone who is abandoned, mocked, and physically tortured. It speaks of being surrounded by enemies, having hands and feet pierced, and even describes the dividing of clothing, which is exactly what happened to Jesus during His crucifixion (Matthew 27:35). What's remarkable is that David wrote these words centuries before the Roman Empire, and crucifixion wasn't even a method of execution during his time. Yet, through the inspiration of God, David described in detail what would happen to the Messiah. When Jesus was crucified, these prophecies were fulfilled down to the smallest detail, showing that His death was not just a tragic event, but a key moment in God's plan of redemption.

The crucifixion also fulfills the prophecies about the suffering servant in Isaiah 53, another powerful example of how the Old Testament pointed forward to the cross. Isaiah 53 speaks of a servant who would bear the sins of many, be wounded for our transgressions, and by His stripes, we would be healed. This prophecy describes how the Messiah would not only suffer physically but also carry the weight of humanity's sins. When Jesus was nailed to the cross, He wasn't just enduring physical pain—He was taking upon Himself the punishment for the sins of the world. This is why His death is so significant. It wasn't just the execution of a man—it was the fulfillment of God's promise to save His people from their sins.

The crucifixion at Calvary is also significant because it shows how Jesus fulfilled the role of the Passover lamb, another prophetic symbol found in the Old Testament. During the first Passover in Egypt, God commanded the Israelites to sacrifice a lamb and put its blood on the doorposts of their homes. This blood served as a sign, and when the angel of death passed through Egypt, it "passed over" the homes that were marked by the blood, sparing the firstborn sons inside (Exodus 12:13). This event foreshadowed what would happen at Calvary. Jesus is often referred to as the Lamb of God (John 1:29), and just as the blood of the Passover lamb saved the Israelites from death, the blood of Jesus saves us from eternal death. When Jesus was crucified, He became the perfect sacrifice, the Lamb who was slain to take away the sins of the world. His death fulfilled the deeper meaning of Passover, showing that God's plan of salvation was not just for the Israelites but for all people.

The prophetic significance of Calvary doesn't stop at the details of Jesus' suffering and death—it also includes the victory that His crucifixion achieved. In Genesis 3:15, after Adam and Eve had sinned, God made a promise that one day the seed of the woman would crush the head of the serpent, symbolizing the defeat of Satan and the power of sin. This is often referred to as the "first gospel" because it is the first hint of God's plan to defeat sin and evil. Jesus' death on the cross was the fulfillment of this promise. Through His death and resurrection, Jesus triumphed over sin, death, and Satan, fulfilling the prophecy given in Genesis and securing victory for all who believe in Him. The cross, which seemed like a symbol of defeat, was actually the place where God's ultimate victory was won. This is why Christians celebrate the cross—not as a tragic event but as the moment when God's salvation plan was accomplished.

The crucifixion at Calvary also fulfilled the prophecy of a new covenant between God and humanity. In Jeremiah 31:31-34, God promised that He would establish a new covenant with His people, one that would not be based on the law written on stone tablets but written on their hearts. This new covenant would bring forgiveness of sins and a close, personal relationship with God. When Jesus instituted the Last Supper before His crucifixion, He spoke of this new covenant, saying that His blood would be shed for the forgiveness of sins (Matthew 26:28). His death on the cross was the moment when this new covenant was put into effect. No longer would people have to offer animal sacrifices or follow a long list of rules to be right with God. Through Jesus' death, the way was opened for all people to come to God in faith, receive forgiveness, and have a personal relationship with Him.

Another prophecy fulfilled by Jesus' crucifixion was the promise that the Messiah would be rejected by His own people. In Psalm 118:22, it says, "The stone which the builders rejected has become the cornerstone." This prophecy was fulfilled when the Jewish leaders rejected Jesus as the Messiah and handed Him over to the Romans to be crucified. Despite their rejection, Jesus became the cornerstone of God's salvation plan. His death and resurrection became the foundation of the Christian faith, and through Him, people from all nations and backgrounds are invited into the family of God. This rejection was part of God's plan all along, showing that even when things seem to go wrong, God is in control, and His purposes will always be fulfilled.

The prophetic significance of Calvary also points to the future. The Bible tells us that Jesus' death and resurrection were not the end of the story. In fact, they marked the beginning of a new era in God's plan for the world. In the book of Revelation, we see a vision of the future where Jesus, the Lamb who was slain, is worshiped by people from every nation and tribe (Revelation 5:9). His death on the cross was the event that made this future possible. Because of what happened at Calvary, the door is open for all people to be forgiven, reconciled to God, and become part of His eternal kingdom. The cross is not just a symbol of the past—it is a sign of the future, where God's plan of salvation will be fully realized when Jesus returns to make all things new.

In conclusion, the crucifixion at Calvary was not just a historical event—it was the fulfillment of God's salvation plan that had been foretold in Scripture for centuries. From the prophecies in Psalm 22 and Isaiah 53 to the promises of the new covenant and the defeat of Satan, every detail of Jesus' death on the cross was part of God's divine plan to rescue humanity from sin and death. The prophetic significance of Calvary shows us that God is faithful to His promises and that His plan for the world is both perfect and unstoppable. Jesus' death on the cross fulfilled the Old Testament prophecies in remarkable ways, demonstrating that He is the promised Messiah, the Savior of the world. Through His sacrifice, we are offered forgiveness, reconciliation with God, and the hope of eternal life. The cross stands as a testament to the fact that God's plan for salvation was not an afterthought or a backup plan—it was His intention all along, and it was fulfilled perfectly at Calvary. This is why the crucifixion holds such powerful meaning for Christians—it is the place where God's love, justice, and faithfulness all come together to offer salvation to the world. The cross is a symbol of suffering, yes, but even more, it is a symbol of hope, victory, and the fulfillment of God's promises. Through Jesus' death at Calvary, God's plan of salvation was accomplished, and all who believe in Him are invited to share in the blessings of that plan for eternity.

Chapter 10 - Path to Eternal Life

The path to eternal life is one of the most important messages in the Christian faith, and it centers on one incredible event: Jesus' sacrifice at Calvary. Through His death on the cross, Jesus opened the door for people to receive eternal life, and this gift is available to anyone who believes in Him. John 3:16, one of the most well-known verses in the Bible, says, "For God so loved the world that He gave His only begotten Son, that whosoever believeth in Him should not perish but have everlasting life." This verse explains the heart of God's plan for humanity. Out of His deep love for us, God sent His Son, Jesus, to take on the punishment for our sins by dying on the cross. His death wasn't just an ordinary death—it was the ultimate sacrifice that made it possible for us to be forgiven of our sins and have eternal life with God. Eternal life means much more than just living forever; it means living in a relationship with God, both now and for all eternity, in a place where there is no more suffering, pain, or death. This promise of eternal life is what gives Christians hope, and it is the central message of the gospel—the good news that Jesus' death at Calvary was the key to opening the way to eternal life for all who believe.

But what does it mean to believe in Jesus and to receive eternal life? To believe in Jesus is not just to know about Him or agree with the facts about His life. It means trusting in Him as your Savior and putting your faith in what He did on the cross. When Jesus died on the cross, He took the punishment for the sins of the whole world. Sin is anything that goes against God's will, and it separates us from God. Every person has sinned, and because of that, we all deserve to be separated from God forever. The Bible tells us that the wages of sin is death (Romans 6:23), which means that the penalty for sin is both physical death and eternal separation from God. But God, in His great love and mercy, didn't want to leave us in that hopeless state. That's why He sent Jesus to be the sacrifice that would take away the sins of the world. By dying on the cross,

Jesus paid the price for our sins, and by believing in Him, we are forgiven and receive the gift of eternal life. This is why the cross is such a powerful symbol for Christians—it represents the moment when Jesus made it possible for us to be saved and to have a future with God that never ends.

Eternal life isn't something we can earn or achieve on our own. It's a gift that is freely given by God to those who believe in Jesus. No matter how hard we try to be good, we can never be good enough to earn eternal life. Our good deeds can never cancel out our sins, and no amount of effort can bridge the gap between us and God. This is why Jesus' sacrifice is so important. He did what we could never do for ourselves—He lived a perfect, sinless life, and then He took the punishment for our sins by dying in our place. When we believe in Jesus, we are accepting the gift of forgiveness that He offers, and in doing so, we are given eternal life. This means that our sins are wiped away, and we are no longer separated from God. Instead, we are brought into a relationship with Him that will last forever. This relationship with God is the true meaning of eternal life. It's not just about living forever; it's about living in the presence of God, experiencing His love, peace, and joy for all eternity.

One of the most amazing things about the path to eternal life is that it is open to everyone. John 3:16 says, "Whosoever believes in Him"—this means that anyone, no matter who they are or what they have done, can receive eternal life by believing in Jesus. It doesn't matter where you come from, how many mistakes you've made, or how far you feel from God—Jesus' sacrifice at Calvary was for all people, and His offer of eternal life is for everyone. Sometimes people feel like they are too bad or have messed up too many times for God to forgive them, but the Bible makes it clear that Jesus' death on the cross was enough to cover all sins. There is no sin too great for God's grace. When Jesus died on the cross, He took the punishment for every sin—past, present, and future—and because of that, anyone who turns to Him in faith can be forgiven and receive eternal life. This is what makes the message of the gospel such good news—it is an invitation to everyone, offering hope, forgiveness, and the promise of eternal life with God.

The path to eternal life through Jesus is also a path of freedom. Sin has a way of trapping people, making them feel guilty, ashamed, and stuck in patterns of bad behavior. But when we believe in Jesus and accept His gift of eternal life, we are set free from the power of sin. The Bible tells us that if anyone is in

Christ, they are a new creation (2 Corinthians 5:17). This means that when we put our faith in Jesus, we are given a fresh start. Our past sins are forgiven, and we are no longer bound by guilt and shame. We are free to live the life that God created us to live—a life of love, joy, and peace in a relationship with Him. This doesn't mean that life will always be easy or that we will never make mistakes again, but it does mean that we are no longer controlled by sin. Jesus' death and resurrection broke the power of sin and death, and because of that, we can live in the freedom of God's grace, knowing that we are forgiven and that our future is secure.

The path to eternal life is also a path of hope. In a world that is often filled with pain, suffering, and uncertainty, the promise of eternal life gives Christians hope for the future. The Bible tells us that one day, Jesus will return, and when He does, He will make all things new. There will be no more death, no more sorrow, no more pain, and no more sin. Those who believe in Jesus will live forever with God in a place where everything is perfect and there is only love, peace, and joy. This is the ultimate hope of the Christian faith—that through Jesus, we are not only saved from our sins, but we are also given the promise of eternal life in a new heaven and a new earth. This hope gives meaning and purpose to our lives now, knowing that no matter what happens, we have a future with God that will never end. It gives Christians the strength to endure difficult times, knowing that this life is not all there is, and that something far greater is waiting for them.

Eternal life doesn't just begin after we die—it begins the moment we believe in Jesus. When we put our faith in Him, we are brought into a relationship with God that starts now and continues for all eternity. This means that we don't have to wait until we get to heaven to experience the benefits of eternal life. Right now, we can experience God's love, peace, and joy in our lives. We can know Him personally and have a relationship with Him that is filled with meaning and purpose. This is one of the most incredible things about eternal life—it's not just about the future; it's about the present, too. When we believe in Jesus, our lives are changed here and now. We are given a new perspective, new purpose, and new hope as we walk with God each day.

The path to eternal life is a gift, and it is offered to everyone, but it requires a response. The Bible tells us that we must repent of our sins and believe in Jesus in order to receive eternal life. Repentance means turning away from sin and turning toward God. It means acknowledging that we have sinned and that we need God's forgiveness. Belief in Jesus means trusting in Him as our Savior, the one who took the punishment for our sins on the cross. When we repent and believe in Jesus, we are forgiven, and we receive the gift of eternal life. This is why the message of the gospel is so urgent—because it is an invitation to everyone to turn to Jesus and receive the gift of eternal life. The Bible says that today is the day of salvation (2 Corinthians 6:2), meaning that we don't have to wait or hesitate. God is offering us the gift of eternal life right now, and all we have to do is accept it by believing in Jesus.

In conclusion, the path to eternal life is found through Jesus' sacrifice at Calvary. By believing in Him, we are forgiven of our sins and given the gift of eternal life. This gift is available to everyone, no matter who they are or what they've done. It is a gift of grace, freely given out of God's love for us. Eternal life is not something we can earn or achieve on our own—it is a gift that comes through faith in Jesus. This eternal life is more than just living forever; it is living in a relationship with God, both now and for all eternity. It is a life of freedom from sin, a life of hope for the future, and a life of peace, joy, and love in the presence of God. The path to eternal life is open to all who will turn to Jesus in faith, and it is the greatest gift anyone could ever receive. Through His death on the cross, Jesus made a way for us to be saved, and by believing in Him, we can have the assurance that we will live forever with God. This is the incredible promise of the gospel—the good news that Jesus' sacrifice at Calvary was the key to opening the way to eternal life for all who believe.

Chapter 11 - Place of Suffering

Calvary was a place of unimaginable suffering, and it is where Jesus Christ endured an immense amount of pain for the sake of humanity. This suffering was not just physical, though that alone was beyond what most people could imagine. Jesus faced emotional rejection and spiritual anguish as well, making Calvary a moment of incredible sacrifice and heartache. In Matthew 27:46, we read one of the most heart-wrenching statements ever recorded: "My God, my God, why have you forsaken me?" These words, spoken by Jesus as He hung on the cross, reflect the depth of His suffering in that moment. He was not only enduring the excruciating pain of crucifixion, but He also experienced a deep, agonizing sense of separation from God. This separation was part of the spiritual suffering He took on as He bore the sins of the world.

The physical suffering that Jesus endured at Calvary was brutal beyond description. Crucifixion was a method of execution designed to inflict maximum pain and humiliation. Jesus was flogged before being nailed to the cross, and Roman scourging was a horrific punishment. The whip, embedded with shards of bone or metal, would have torn through His skin, leaving deep wounds and immense bleeding. After this beating, Jesus was forced to carry His cross to the place of execution. Exhausted, dehydrated, and in agonizing pain, He struggled under the weight of the heavy wooden cross. Once at Calvary, His hands and feet were nailed to the cross, and He was lifted up to hang, enduring hours of agonizing pain as His body was wracked with suffering. Every breath He took would have been painful, as crucifixion made breathing incredibly difficult. The physical pain was unimaginable, and yet this was only one part of the suffering Jesus faced.

Emotional rejection was another layer of the suffering Jesus experienced at Calvary. Throughout His life and ministry, Jesus was misunderstood, mocked, and rejected by many. At the time of His crucifixion, the crowds that once followed Him were now shouting for His death. He was abandoned by many of His closest followers, including His disciples, who had fled in fear. Even Peter, one of His closest friends, had denied knowing Him three times. The very people Jesus came to save were now calling for His crucifixion, mocking Him as He hung on the cross. The soldiers who nailed Him to the cross and those who passed by hurled insults at Him, saying, "If you are the Son of God, come down from the cross!" (Matthew 27:40). The rejection He faced from humanity, the people He loved and had come to rescue, added deep emotional pain to His already unbearable physical suffering. The loneliness and sense of abandonment in these moments were real and heavy.

Yet, the most profound suffering Jesus endured at Calvary was spiritual. When Jesus cried out, "My God, my God, why have you forsaken me?" it was the cry of someone who was experiencing the full weight of the world's sin on His shoulders. Jesus had lived His entire life in perfect communion with God the Father, but at that moment on the cross, He felt the separation that sin causes between humanity and God. As He bore the sins of the world, He experienced the spiritual separation that sin brings, a separation that He had never known before. This spiritual anguish was perhaps the greatest suffering of all. Jesus, who had never sinned, was taking on the punishment for all the sins of humanity—past, present, and future. The weight of this sin was crushing, and for the first time, Jesus experienced the forsakenness that sin brings.

This unimaginable suffering that Jesus endured at Calvary was not without purpose. He willingly went through this agony out of love for humanity. Jesus endured the cross so that we would not have to face the consequences of our sins. The physical, emotional, and spiritual suffering that He took on was the punishment that we deserved. He stood in our place, taking the wrath of God upon Himself so that we could be forgiven and reconciled to God. Calvary, therefore, was not just a place of suffering—it was the place where God's love for humanity was demonstrated in the most profound way. Jesus' suffering was the cost of our redemption, and because of His sacrifice, we can have life and forgiveness.

In addition to this, Jesus' suffering at Calvary fulfilled the prophecies of the Old Testament. The prophet Isaiah had foretold of a suffering servant who would be "pierced for our transgressions" and "crushed for our iniquities" (Isaiah 53:5). Jesus' suffering was the fulfillment of God's plan for salvation.

His suffering was not meaningless; it was part of a greater purpose. Through His suffering, Jesus opened the way for humanity to be restored to a right relationship with God. His death on the cross made it possible for us to receive forgiveness for our sins and the hope of eternal life.

In conclusion, Calvary was truly a place of unimaginable suffering. Jesus endured incredible physical pain, emotional rejection, and deep spiritual anguish as He took on the sins of the world. His suffering was the price He paid for our salvation, and it was driven by His love for humanity. The pain and rejection He experienced at Calvary were overwhelming, but they were not without purpose. Through His suffering, Jesus provided a way for us to be forgiven and reconciled to God. His suffering reminds us of the seriousness of sin, but it also shows us the depth of God's love and the lengths He was willing to go to save us. The suffering Jesus endured at Calvary was immense, but it was the very suffering that made our salvation possible. Through His sacrifice, we are offered life, hope, and a restored relationship with God.

Chapter 13 - Prefigured in Passover

The sacrifice that took place at Calvary, where Jesus Christ gave His life for the sins of humanity, was not an isolated event. It was part of a divine plan that had been foreshadowed and prefigured centuries earlier in the story of the Passover, one of the most significant events in the history of the Israelites. Calvary's sacrifice was prefigured in the Passover lamb, and this symbolism powerfully points to Jesus as the Lamb of God who takes away the sin of the world, just as John the Baptist declared in John 1:29. To understand the connection between the Passover and Jesus' death on the cross, we need to look back to the story of the Exodus in the Old Testament, where God's plan for salvation was first revealed through a powerful act of deliverance.

In the book of Exodus, we learn about the Israelites who were enslaved in Egypt for over 400 years. They cried out to God for deliverance, and God responded by raising up Moses to lead them to freedom. But before Pharaoh, the ruler of Egypt, would let the Israelites go, God sent a series of ten plagues upon Egypt. The final and most devastating plague was the death of the firstborn in every household. However, God provided a way for the Israelites to be spared from this judgment. He commanded them to take a lamb without blemish, slaughter it, and put its blood on the doorposts of their homes. When the angel of death passed through Egypt, it would "pass over" the houses that were marked by the blood of the lamb, sparing the firstborn in those homes from death. This event became known as the Passover, and it was a defining moment in the history of Israel. It was through the blood of the lamb that the Israelites were saved from death and freed from slavery.

The Passover lamb was a powerful symbol of God's deliverance, and it pointed forward to an even greater deliverance that would come through Jesus Christ. Just as the blood of the lamb saved the Israelites from physical death, the blood of Jesus, the true Lamb of God, saves humanity from spiritual death.

Jesus' sacrifice at Calvary fulfilled the deeper meaning of the Passover, offering not just temporary physical salvation, but eternal spiritual salvation. When John the Baptist saw Jesus, he declared, "Behold, the Lamb of God, who takes away the sin of the world!" (John 1:29). This statement directly connects Jesus to the Passover lamb, showing that He is the ultimate sacrifice that would bring about the forgiveness of sins for all people. The Passover lamb in the Old Testament was a foreshadowing, or a prefigurement, of what Jesus would do on the cross. The lamb had to be spotless, without any blemish, symbolizing purity and perfection, and Jesus was the only one who was without sin, making Him the perfect sacrifice.

At Calvary, Jesus became the Lamb of God in the truest sense. Just as the Passover lamb was slain and its blood applied to the doorposts to save the Israelites, Jesus was slain, and His blood was shed to save all of humanity from the consequences of sin. In the same way that the blood of the Passover lamb saved the Israelites from death, the blood of Jesus saves us from spiritual death and separation from God. The imagery of the Passover is rich with meaning, and it helps us understand the significance of what Jesus accomplished on the cross. His sacrifice was not just a random act of love—it was the fulfillment of a divine plan that had been set in motion long before. The Passover was a picture of what was to come, and at Calvary, that picture became a reality.

The parallels between the Passover and Jesus' sacrifice at Calvary are striking. In the Passover, the lamb's blood had to be applied to the doorposts of each home, and only those who were covered by the blood were saved. In the same way, Jesus' sacrifice at Calvary is available to all, but it must be personally accepted. It's not enough to simply know about Jesus or His death on the cross; each person must make the decision to accept His sacrifice for themselves, to be "covered" by His blood, so to speak. This is how we receive the forgiveness of sins and the gift of eternal life. Just as the Israelites had to take action by applying the blood of the lamb to their doorposts, we must take action by placing our faith in Jesus and accepting His sacrifice on our behalf.

Another important parallel is the idea of deliverance from slavery. The Passover marked the beginning of the Israelites' journey out of slavery in Egypt and toward freedom in the Promised Land. In the same way, Jesus' sacrifice at Calvary marks the beginning of our deliverance from the slavery of sin. Sin enslaves us, trapping us in guilt, shame, and separation from God. But through

Jesus' death and resurrection, we are set free from the power of sin and death. Just as the Israelites were set free from their physical bondage, we are set free from spiritual bondage through the blood of Jesus. This freedom is not just a future promise; it's something we can experience here and now as we live in the freedom that comes from being forgiven and reconciled to God.

The timing of Jesus' crucifixion also ties in with the symbolism of the Passover. Jesus was crucified during the Passover festival in Jerusalem, and this was no coincidence. It was a deliberate part of God's plan. As the Jewish people were celebrating the Passover and remembering how God had delivered their ancestors from slavery in Egypt, Jesus was becoming the ultimate Passover Lamb, providing deliverance from sin and death for all people. His death during Passover was a powerful reminder that the true meaning of the festival was being fulfilled in Him. The timing of these events shows how God's plan for salvation was woven throughout history, with every detail pointing to the moment when Jesus would offer Himself as the sacrifice for the sins of the world.

The Passover was also a communal event. The Israelites celebrated it together as a people, and they were instructed to remember it and celebrate it every year as a way of commemorating what God had done for them. In the same way, Christians gather together to remember and celebrate Jesus' sacrifice through the practice of communion, also known as the Lord's Supper. During the Last Supper, which took place the night before Jesus was crucified, He took the bread and the cup and told His disciples that these elements represented His body and His blood, which would be given for them. This act of remembrance connects directly to the Passover meal, but instead of looking back to the Exodus from Egypt, it looks forward to the ultimate deliverance that Jesus would provide through His death on the cross. Every time Christians take communion, they are reminded of the sacrifice of the Lamb of God, who takes away the sin of the world, and they participate in the ongoing story of God's salvation plan.

The connection between the Passover and Calvary also teaches us something about the nature of God's love and justice. In the Passover, God provided a way for the Israelites to escape the judgment that was coming upon Egypt. In the same way, at Calvary, God provided a way for us to escape the judgment that we deserve because of our sin. Sin separates us from God, and the Bible tells us that the wages of sin is death (Romans 6:23). But just as God provided the blood of the Passover lamb to save the Israelites from death, He provided the blood of Jesus to save us from eternal death. This shows us that God's love and justice work together perfectly. He is a God of justice, who cannot ignore sin, but He is also a God of love, who made a way for us to be forgiven and reconciled to Him through the sacrifice of His Son.

In conclusion, the sacrifice at Calvary was prefigured in the Passover, and this connection reveals the depth and beauty of God's plan for salvation. The Passover lamb in the Old Testament was a foreshadowing of Jesus, the Lamb of God who takes away the sin of the world. Just as the blood of the Passover lamb saved the Israelites from death and delivered them from slavery, the blood of Jesus saves us from spiritual death and delivers us from the slavery of sin. His sacrifice at Calvary fulfilled the deeper meaning of the Passover, offering eternal salvation to all who believe in Him. The parallels between the Passover and Calvary show us that Jesus' death on the cross was not a random event, but the fulfillment of a divine plan that had been in motion since the beginning of time. It reminds us that God's love and justice work together perfectly, and that through Jesus' sacrifice, we are offered the gift of eternal life and the freedom to live in a restored relationship with God. The Passover was a symbol of temporary deliverance, but Jesus' sacrifice at Calvary is the ultimate act of deliverance that brings eternal life to all who believe.

Chapter 14 - Place of Reconciliation

Calvary is known as the place where one of the most important events in the Christian faith took place: the reconciliation of humanity with God through Jesus Christ. At Calvary, Jesus accomplished something extraordinary by bridging the gap that sin had created between people and God, and this act of reconciliation is one of the central themes of the gospel. In 2 Corinthians 5:18-19, we read, "All this is from God, who reconciled us to himself through Christ and gave us the ministry of reconciliation: that God was reconciling the world to himself in Christ, not counting people's sins against them." This verse captures the heart of what happened at Calvary: Jesus' death on the cross was the means by which God reconciled humanity to Himself, healing the broken relationship caused by sin. Reconciliation is a word that means to restore a broken relationship, to bring two sides together again, and at Calvary, that's exactly what Jesus did for all of us. He restored the relationship between humanity and God that had been damaged by sin, and through His sacrifice, He made it possible for us to be close to God once again.

To fully appreciate the significance of this reconciliation, we need to understand why it was necessary in the first place. The Bible teaches that sin entered the world through the disobedience of Adam and Eve in the Garden of Eden. From that moment, humanity's relationship with God was broken. Sin is anything that goes against God's will and His perfect, holy nature. It separates us from God because God is pure and without sin, and sin cannot exist in His presence. The Bible describes sin as creating a barrier or a gap between people and God. This gap is something that no amount of good deeds, religious practices, or self-effort can fix. The separation caused by sin is so deep that only God Himself could bridge it. Sin leads to death, not just physical death but spiritual death—eternal separation from God. This is the great problem that humanity faces: without reconciliation, we are cut off from the source of life, love, and hope, which is God. We need to be reconciled to Him, but because of our sin, we are incapable of doing it on our own.

That's where Jesus comes in. At Calvary, Jesus took the first step in bridging the gap between humanity and God. He did what we could never do for ourselves—He offered Himself as a sacrifice to pay for our sins. The Bible says that the wages of sin is death (Romans 6:23), meaning that the just penalty for sin is death and separation from God. But Jesus, who was without sin, took our place. He died the death that we deserved so that we wouldn't have to. In doing so, He removed the barrier of sin that separated us from God. His death on the cross was the ultimate act of love and mercy, and it was the only way that humanity could be reconciled to God. Jesus is described in the Bible as the "mediator" between God and people (1 Timothy 2:5), and at Calvary, He fulfilled that role perfectly. He stood in the gap, so to speak, and made a way for us to be brought back into a relationship with God.

This act of reconciliation was not just for a few people; it was for the entire world. In 2 Corinthians 5:19, it says that God was reconciling the world to Himself in Christ, not counting people's sins against them. This means that the offer of reconciliation is available to everyone. No matter who you are, where you come from, or what you've done, Jesus' sacrifice at Calvary was for you. He died for all of humanity, offering forgiveness and reconciliation to anyone who would accept it. This is one of the most amazing things about the gospel—it's an open invitation to all people to be reconciled to God. The gap that sin created is not too big for God to bridge, and through Jesus, He has made a way for everyone to come back to Him. It doesn't matter how far you feel from God or how much you think you've messed up—Jesus' death on the cross is powerful enough to reconcile even the worst of sinners.

At Calvary, Jesus didn't just make reconciliation possible—He also demonstrated what it looks like. His death on the cross was the ultimate example of selfless love and forgiveness. As He hung on the cross, suffering in unimaginable pain, He prayed for those who were crucifying Him, saying, "Father, forgive them, for they know not what they do" (Luke 23:34). In this moment, Jesus showed the world what it means to seek reconciliation, even with those who have wronged you. His prayer for forgiveness was not just for the Roman soldiers who were physically crucifying Him, but for all of humanity. We are all guilty of sin, and it was our sin that put Jesus on the cross.

Yet, in His great love, Jesus chose to forgive us and to take the punishment for our sins upon Himself. This is the heart of reconciliation: forgiveness and the willingness to restore a broken relationship, even at great personal cost.

The reconciliation that Jesus accomplished at Calvary is not just about being forgiven of our sins—it's also about being brought into a new relationship with God. Before we are reconciled, sin separates us from God, making us distant from Him. But through Jesus, that distance is closed, and we are invited into a close, personal relationship with God. The Bible tells us that through Jesus, we are adopted into God's family as His children (Galatians 4:4-7). This means that reconciliation is not just about getting rid of the bad things (our sins); it's about gaining something incredible—a restored relationship with God where we can know Him, love Him, and experience His love for us. When we are reconciled to God, we are no longer His enemies, no longer separated from Him by sin. Instead, we are His beloved children, and we can enjoy the fullness of life that comes from being in a relationship with Him.

Another important aspect of reconciliation is that it brings peace. The Bible speaks of Jesus as the "Prince of Peace" (Isaiah 9:6), and at Calvary, He brought peace between humanity and God. Before we are reconciled, there is conflict between us and God because of our sin. But through Jesus' sacrifice, that conflict is resolved, and we are brought into a state of peace with God. This peace is not just a feeling; it's a deep, spiritual reality. It means that we are no longer under the judgment of sin, no longer separated from God, and no longer distant from His love. Instead, we are at peace with Him, knowing that our sins have been forgiven and that we are in right standing with Him. This peace also gives us security and confidence in our relationship with God. We no longer have to live in fear of being rejected by Him or worry about whether we've done enough to earn His favor. Through Jesus, we are reconciled, and that reconciliation is secure.

The reconciliation that Jesus accomplished at Calvary also has implications for how we relate to others. In 2 Corinthians 5:18, we are told that God has given us the "ministry of reconciliation." This means that just as God has reconciled us to Himself through Christ, we are called to be agents of reconciliation in the world. This involves sharing the good news of Jesus with others so that they, too, can be reconciled to God. But it also means seeking reconciliation in our relationships with other people. Jesus' death on the cross is the ultimate example of forgiveness and reconciliation, and as His followers, we are called to reflect that in our own lives. This might mean forgiving someone who has wronged us, seeking to mend a broken relationship, or being a peacemaker in situations of conflict. Reconciliation is not just something we receive from God; it's something we are called to extend to others.

At Calvary, the reconciliation between humanity and God was accomplished once and for all. Jesus' death on the cross was a one-time event, but its impact stretches across all of time. Because of what Jesus did at Calvary, we have the opportunity to be reconciled to God, no matter when or where we live. His sacrifice was sufficient to cover all of humanity's sins—past, present, and future. This means that the offer of reconciliation is always open. It's never too late to be reconciled to God, and His arms are always open, ready to welcome us back into a relationship with Him. The reconciliation that Jesus offers is complete and permanent. Once we are reconciled to God through faith in Jesus, nothing can separate us from His love (Romans 8:38-39). This is the hope and security that comes from being reconciled to God through Christ.

In conclusion, Calvary is the place of reconciliation, where Jesus Christ bridged the gap that sin had created between humanity and God. Through His death on the cross, Jesus took the punishment for our sins, removed the barrier of sin, and made it possible for us to be restored to a right relationship with God. This act of reconciliation was driven by God's incredible love for us, and it is available to everyone who believes in Jesus. The reconciliation that Jesus accomplished at Calvary brings peace, forgiveness, and a new relationship with God where we are no longer separated from Him by sin. Instead, we are brought into His family as His beloved children. This reconciliation also calls us to be agents of reconciliation in the world, sharing the good news of Jesus with others and seeking to restore broken relationships in our own lives. The reconciliation that Jesus offers is complete and secure, giving us the hope of eternal life and the assurance that we are forever loved and accepted by God.

Chapter 15 - Power Over Death

The crucifixion of Jesus Christ at Calvary is one of the most powerful and significant events in all of human history. It was not just an act of love or sacrifice—it was the moment when Jesus achieved victory over death itself, offering hope and the promise of resurrection to all who believe. This victory over death is the foundation of the Christian faith, and it transforms the way we understand life, death, and eternity. In 1 Corinthians 15:55-57, the Apostle Paul triumphantly declares, "O death, where is thy sting? O grave, where is thy victory? The sting of death is sin; and the strength of sin is the law. But thanks be to God, which giveth us the victory through our Lord Jesus Christ." These words capture the essence of what Jesus accomplished through His death and resurrection—He took away the power of death and gave humanity the gift of eternal life.

To truly appreciate the power of Jesus' victory over death, we need to understand why death is such a significant problem in the first place. Death entered the world because of sin. In the Garden of Eden, when Adam and Eve disobeyed God, they introduced sin into the world, and with sin came death. The Bible tells us that the wages of sin is death (Romans 6:23), meaning that the consequence of sin is both physical death and eternal separation from God. Every person who has ever lived is affected by sin, and because of that, death is something we all face. It is the ultimate enemy, the final frontier that no one can escape on their own. For centuries, people have feared death, knowing that it is the inevitable end of life. It brings loss, sorrow, and pain, and it has often been seen as an unconquerable force. But Jesus' crucifixion and resurrection changed all of that. Through His death on the cross, Jesus took on the penalty for sin, and through His resurrection, He defeated death once and for all.

When Jesus was crucified, it looked like death had won. His followers watched as He was brutally nailed to a cross and died a slow, agonizing death.

His body was placed in a tomb, and for those who loved Him, it must have seemed like all hope was lost. Death, which had claimed countless lives throughout history, now seemed to have claimed Jesus, too. But three days later, everything changed. Jesus rose from the dead, proving that death could not hold Him. His resurrection was the proof of His power over death and the fulfillment of the promise that He had made to His followers. Before He died, Jesus had told His disciples that He would rise again, but they didn't fully understand what that meant. When Jesus stepped out of the tomb, it became clear—He had conquered death, not just for Himself, but for everyone who believes in Him.

The resurrection of Jesus is central to the Christian faith because it shows that death is not the end. For those who believe in Jesus, death no longer has the final word. Jesus' victory over death means that we, too, can have victory over death through Him. This is the incredible promise of the gospel—eternal life with God. Jesus' resurrection was the first of its kind, but it was also the guarantee that everyone who puts their faith in Him will experience resurrection as well. Just as Jesus was raised from the dead, those who believe in Him will be raised to eternal life. This is the hope of the resurrection, and it changes everything about how we view life and death. Death is no longer something to be feared because, through Jesus, it has been defeated.

The Bible describes Jesus as the "firstfruits" of the resurrection (1 Corinthians 15:20). This means that His resurrection is the first of many to come. When a farmer gathers the firstfruits of the harvest, it is a sign that there is more to come, and in the same way, Jesus' resurrection is a sign that all who believe in Him will one day be raised from the dead. This promise gives Christians incredible hope, especially in the face of death. Even though we still experience physical death in this life, we know that it is not the end. Because of Jesus' victory over death, we have the promise of eternal life, where there will be no more pain, no more suffering, and no more death. The resurrection offers us the assurance that death is not something to fear, but rather a gateway to a new and eternal life with God.

One of the most powerful aspects of Jesus' victory over death is that it also brings freedom from the fear of death. Throughout history, people have lived in fear of dying, unsure of what comes after death or if there is anything at all beyond the grave. But Jesus' resurrection provides a clear answer to that question. His resurrection shows that there is life after death, and for those who believe in Him, it is a life filled with peace, joy, and the presence of God. The fear of death no longer has to control our lives because Jesus has already won the victory over it. When we put our faith in Him, we are no longer bound by the fear of the unknown. We can face death with confidence, knowing that it is not the end, but the beginning of eternal life with God.

Jesus' victory over death also brings hope in the midst of suffering and loss. One of the hardest parts of life is dealing with the death of loved ones. It brings deep sorrow and grief, and it can feel like an unbearable loss. But because of Jesus' resurrection, we have hope even in the face of death. For those who have put their faith in Jesus, death is not the final goodbye—it is a temporary separation. We know that one day, we will be reunited with our loved ones in the presence of God, and we will never have to experience the pain of loss again. This hope sustains us in times of grief and gives us the strength to endure even the hardest moments of life. The resurrection of Jesus is a promise that we will see our loved ones again and that death does not have the final say.

The power of Jesus' victory over death also transforms the way we live our lives now. Because we know that death has been defeated and eternal life is promised to us, we can live with purpose, courage, and hope. We no longer have to live in fear of the future because we know that our future is secure in Christ. The promise of resurrection gives us a new perspective on life. Instead of living for temporary things that will one day fade away, we can live for what truly matters—our relationship with God and the eternal life He offers. This changes our priorities, our values, and the way we approach every day. We can live with boldness and confidence, knowing that nothing, not even death, can separate us from the love of God.

Another incredible aspect of Jesus' victory over death is that it is available to everyone. The promise of resurrection is not just for a select few; it is for all who believe in Jesus. No matter who you are, where you come from, or what you have done, the victory over death that Jesus achieved at Calvary is available to you. His death and resurrection were for the entire world, offering the gift of eternal life to anyone who will accept it. This is one of the most beautiful things about the gospel—it is an open invitation to everyone. Jesus' victory over death is a gift that is freely given to all who believe in Him, and it changes everything about how we view life, death, and eternity.

The resurrection of Jesus also brings a sense of justice and restoration. In a world filled with pain, suffering, and injustice, the resurrection is a promise that one day, everything will be made right. Jesus' victory over death is not just about individual salvation; it is about the restoration of all creation. The Bible tells us that one day, Jesus will return, and when He does, He will make all things new. There will be no more death, no more pain, and no more suffering. Everything that was broken by sin will be restored, and God's perfect justice will be established. This is the ultimate hope of the resurrection—that through Jesus' victory over death, all of creation will be redeemed and restored to the way it was meant to be.

In conclusion, the crucifixion of Jesus Christ led to His victory over death, and this victory has profound implications for all who believe. Through His death and resurrection, Jesus defeated the power of death, offering the promise of eternal life to everyone who puts their faith in Him. Death, once the ultimate enemy, has been conquered, and for those who believe in Jesus, it is no longer something to be feared. Instead, it is the beginning of a new and eternal life with God. The resurrection of Jesus provides hope in the face of death, comfort in times of grief, and freedom from the fear of the unknown. It also gives us a new perspective on life, allowing us to live with purpose and confidence, knowing that our future is secure in Christ. Jesus' victory over death is available to everyone, and it is the foundation of the Christian faith. Through His resurrection, we are given the promise of eternal life, and we can look forward to a future where death will be no more, and we will live forever in the presence of God. This is the power of the resurrection—the ultimate victory over death, secured by Jesus at Calvary and offered to all who believe.

Chapter 16 - Pinnacle of Obedience

Calvary represents the pinnacle of obedience because it was at this moment that Jesus Christ displayed the ultimate act of submission to God the Father, obeying His will even to the point of death on a cross. In Philippians 2:8, we read, "And being found in fashion as a man, he humbled himself, and became obedient unto death, even the death of the cross." This verse reveals the depth of Jesus' humility and obedience. His entire life was a model of submission to God's will, but it was at Calvary, in His suffering and death, that His obedience reached its highest and most profound point. Jesus' willingness to die on the cross was not just an act of sacrifice; it was the ultimate demonstration of obedience, where He laid aside His own desires and fully embraced the Father's plan for the salvation of humanity. This moment at Calvary is what makes Jesus' obedience the pinnacle of all acts of submission and faithfulness, as He chose to follow God's will, even though it meant enduring unimaginable suffering and death.

To understand the magnitude of Jesus' obedience at Calvary, we must first consider what obedience means in the context of His life and mission. From the beginning of His ministry, Jesus made it clear that His purpose was to do the will of the Father. He often spoke about how He was sent by God not to do His own will, but to carry out the mission that God had given Him. This mission was not easy—it involved teaching people the truth, healing the sick, showing love to the outcasts, and ultimately, sacrificing His life for the sins of the world. Jesus knew that His mission would lead Him to the cross, and yet, He remained obedient to the Father's plan every step of the way. His life was a continuous act of obedience, but it was at Calvary that His obedience was tested to the extreme. In the Garden of Gethsemane, on the night before His crucifixion, Jesus prayed with deep anguish, asking God, "Father, if you are willing, take this cup from me; yet not my will, but yours be done" (Luke 22:42). This moment shows us the inner struggle Jesus faced as He contemplated the suffering that awaited Him. As fully human, Jesus experienced fear, pain, and sorrow, and yet, in His obedience, He surrendered His will to the Father's. He could have chosen to avoid the cross, but He didn't—He chose to obey, even when it meant facing death.

The obedience that Jesus displayed at Calvary was remarkable because it was entirely voluntary. Jesus was not forced to die on the cross; He chose to do so out of love for the Father and for humanity. In John 10:18, Jesus said, "No one takes it from me, but I lay it down of my own accord. I have authority to lay it down and authority to take it up again. This command I received from my Father." This statement makes it clear that Jesus had the power to avoid the cross if He wanted to, but His obedience to the Father's plan was greater than His desire to escape suffering. He willingly laid down His life, demonstrating perfect obedience and submission. This is what makes His sacrifice so powerful—Jesus had every opportunity to walk away from the cross, but He chose obedience because He knew it was the only way to accomplish God's plan of salvation for the world. His decision to obey, even at the cost of His own life, shows the depth of His love for God and for us.

At Calvary, Jesus' obedience was not only about submitting to God's will—it was also about fulfilling the purpose of His life. Jesus came into the world with a clear mission: to save humanity from sin and restore the broken relationship between people and God. This mission could only be accomplished through His death on the cross, where He would take upon Himself the punishment for our sins. The Bible tells us that the wages of sin is death (Romans 6:23), meaning that the consequence of sin is separation from God and eternal death. Every person is guilty of sin, and because of that, we all deserve this punishment. But God, in His great love and mercy, provided a way for us to be saved, and that way was through Jesus' obedient death. Jesus was the only person who lived a sinless life, making Him the perfect sacrifice to take our place. At Calvary, Jesus' obedience meant that He willingly took the punishment for our sins, allowing us to be forgiven and reconciled to God. His obedience was the key to fulfilling God's plan of salvation, and without it, we would still be lost in our sins.

Jesus' obedience at Calvary was also an act of incredible humility. In Philippians 2:6-7, we are told that although Jesus was in the very nature God,

He did not consider equality with God something to be used to His own advantage; instead, He emptied Himself, taking on the form of a servant. This humility is at the heart of Jesus' obedience. Even though He was fully God, Jesus humbled Himself by becoming a man and submitting to the limitations and sufferings of human life. He did not cling to His divine privileges, but instead, He chose to obey the Father's will, even when it meant enduring the shame and agony of the cross. This is what makes Jesus' obedience so extraordinary—He was willing to humble Himself to the lowest point, accepting death on a cross, a form of execution reserved for the worst criminals. His obedience was not driven by pride or self-interest, but by love and humility.

At Calvary, Jesus' obedience was also a demonstration of His complete trust in the Father. Even in the face of death, Jesus trusted that God's plan was good and that His suffering would lead to the ultimate victory over sin and death. This trust was evident in Jesus' final words on the cross, "Father, into your hands I commit my spirit" (Luke 23:46). In His moment of greatest pain and abandonment, Jesus continued to trust the Father's will, knowing that His death would bring about the salvation of the world. His obedience was rooted in His faith in God's perfect plan, and this faith enabled Him to endure the suffering of the cross with the confidence that it would lead to something far greater. Jesus' trust in the Father's plan is an example for all of us, showing us that true obedience is not just about following commands, but about trusting God's wisdom and goodness, even when we don't fully understand His plan.

The obedience that Jesus displayed at Calvary was not just for His own sake—it was for the sake of all humanity. Through His obedient death, Jesus opened the way for us to be saved from our sins and reconciled to God. His obedience brought about the greatest victory in history—the defeat of sin, death, and Satan. In Romans 5:19, Paul explains that just as through one man's disobedience (Adam) many were made sinners, so through the obedience of one man (Jesus) many will be made righteous. This means that Jesus' obedience at Calvary has eternal consequences for all who believe in Him. Because of His obedience, we are offered the gift of righteousness, forgiveness, and eternal life. His obedience was the turning point in the story of humanity's relationship with God, and it is through His obedience that we are able to be saved.

The obedience that Jesus demonstrated at Calvary also sets an example for us to follow. As Christians, we are called to follow in Jesus' footsteps and live lives of obedience to God. Jesus' obedience shows us that following God's will is not always easy—it often requires sacrifice, humility, and self-denial. But it also shows us that obedience leads to victory and blessing. Jesus' obedience brought about the greatest blessing of all—salvation for humanity. In the same way, when we obey God, even in the face of challenges, we can trust that He will use our obedience to bring about good in our lives and in the world. Jesus' obedience at Calvary reminds us that true obedience is motivated by love for God and trust in His plan. It teaches us that obedience is not about seeking our own will, but about submitting to God's will, even when it is difficult.

Another important aspect of Jesus' obedience at Calvary is that it fulfilled the prophecies and promises of the Old Testament. Throughout the Scriptures, God had promised to send a Savior who would redeem His people, and Jesus' death on the cross was the fulfillment of those promises. From the very beginning, God had a plan to save humanity, and Jesus' obedience was the key to making that plan a reality. The prophets had foretold of a suffering servant who would take on the sins of the world and bring salvation, and Jesus fulfilled those prophecies through His obedient death on the cross. His obedience was not just a personal act of devotion to God—it was the fulfillment of a divine plan that had been in motion since the beginning of time.

In conclusion, Calvary represents the pinnacle of obedience, where Jesus Christ perfectly submitted to the will of God the Father, even to the point of death on the cross. His obedience was driven by love for the Father and for humanity, and it was the key to fulfilling God's plan of salvation. Through His obedient sacrifice, Jesus took on the punishment for our sins, reconciled us to God, and opened the way for us to receive forgiveness and eternal life. His obedience at Calvary was not a passive acceptance of suffering—it was an active, deliberate choice to follow God's will, even though it required the greatest sacrifice. Jesus' obedience is the ultimate example for us to follow, showing us that true obedience is motivated by love and trust in God's perfect plan. Calvary stands as a powerful reminder of the importance of obedience, and it teaches us that through obedience, even in the face of great difficulty, God's purposes are fulfilled, and His blessings are poured out. Jesus' obedience at Calvary changed the course of history and offers hope and salvation to all who believe in Him. This is why Calvary is the pinnacle of obedience—the moment when Jesus' perfect submission to God's will brought about the greatest victory of all time.

Chapter 17 - Place of Humiliation

Calvary is known as the place of ultimate humiliation for Jesus Christ, where He was mocked, scorned, and ridiculed by onlookers, yet He endured it all for the sake of humanity. This moment in history, where Jesus willingly suffered such intense humiliation, is central to understanding the depth of His love, His sacrifice, and His purpose. In Mark 15:29-32, we read about the cruel treatment Jesus received as He hung on the cross: "And they that passed by railed on him, wagging their heads, and saying, Ah, thou that destroyest the temple, and buildest it in three days, save thyself, and come down from the cross. Likewise also the chief priests mocking said among themselves with the scribes, He saved others; himself he cannot save. Let Christ the King of Israel descend now from the cross, that we may see and believe." These verses paint a clear picture of the utter humiliation Jesus faced at Calvary. People mocked His claims, insulted His identity, and taunted Him to prove His power by coming down from the cross. But despite this scorn, Jesus did not retaliate or defend Himself. Instead, He endured the humiliation with quiet strength, knowing that His suffering would lead to the salvation of countless souls.

The humiliation Jesus experienced at Calvary was not just a momentary incident—it was part of a pattern of suffering and rejection that He endured throughout His life and ministry. From the time He began His public ministry, Jesus faced opposition from religious leaders, ridicule from skeptics, and rejection from many who could not accept His message. But at Calvary, the intensity of the humiliation reached its peak. The Roman soldiers had already mocked Him before the crucifixion by dressing Him in a purple robe, placing a crown of thorns on His head, and mocking Him as "King of the Jews" (Mark 15:17-20). They beat Him, spit on Him, and knelt in mock worship. Afterward, they led Him to Calvary, where the ultimate humiliation took place. Jesus was crucified between two criminals, treated as if He were a common criminal Himself, though He had done nothing wrong. His body was exposed to the elements, and He was left to die in one of the most degrading and painful ways imaginable.

The physical pain of crucifixion was immense, but the emotional and spiritual humiliation was just as excruciating. As Jesus hung on the cross, struggling to breathe, He was surrounded by people who mocked Him, wagged their heads in disdain, and questioned His power. "If you are the Son of God," they taunted, "come down from the cross!" (Matthew 27:40). Even the religious leaders, who should have been able to recognize who Jesus was, joined in the mockery, saying, "He saved others; Himself He cannot save" (Mark 15:31). These words were intended to mock and belittle Jesus, but in a profound way, they spoke the truth. Jesus chose not to save Himself because He was focused on saving us. His decision to remain on the cross, despite the humiliation, was an act of unparalleled love. He could have called down angels to rescue Him at any moment, but He stayed because He knew that His suffering was the only way to redeem humanity from sin.

What makes the humiliation of Jesus at Calvary even more significant is that He was completely innocent. Unlike the criminals crucified beside Him, Jesus had done nothing wrong. He was sinless, yet He was treated as the worst kind of criminal. This underscores the depth of His sacrifice—He willingly took on the punishment and shame that we deserved. In that moment, Jesus was bearing the weight of the world's sins, and the humiliation He endured was part of that burden. The people who mocked Him did not understand that He was suffering on their behalf. They thought they were ridiculing a man who had failed, but in reality, they were witnessing the greatest act of love and redemption in history.

Jesus' humiliation at Calvary also fulfilled Old Testament prophecies that had foretold the suffering of the Messiah. Isaiah 53:3 describes the Messiah as "despised and rejected by men, a man of sorrows, and acquainted with grief." Jesus' life and death perfectly matched this description. He was despised, rejected, and humiliated by those He came to save. Yet, despite this rejection, He remained obedient to the will of the Father, accepting the humiliation as part of God's plan for salvation. This is what makes Jesus' suffering so profound—He knew the humiliation was coming, but He willingly endured it because of His love for humanity. His willingness to endure such shame and suffering is a testament to the lengths He was willing to go to save us.

The humiliation Jesus faced at Calvary was also deeply spiritual. Beyond the physical pain and the mockery of the crowd, Jesus experienced the spiritual anguish of bearing the sins of the world. For the first time in His eternal existence, Jesus experienced separation from the Father as He took on the sins of humanity. This was the ultimate humiliation for Jesus, who had always lived in perfect communion with God. As He hung on the cross, He cried out, "My God, my God, why have you forsaken me?" (Matthew 27:46). This cry of abandonment reflects the depth of His spiritual suffering. Jesus was experiencing the full weight of sin—our sin—on His shoulders. He was humiliated not only in the eyes of the people around Him but in a deeper, spiritual sense as He took the punishment for sin that we deserved. His willingness to endure this spiritual humiliation shows the depth of His commitment to saving us.

Despite the immense humiliation He faced, Jesus did not retaliate or respond with anger. He could have called down divine judgment on those who mocked Him, but instead, He responded with forgiveness. As He hung on the cross, Jesus prayed, "Father, forgive them, for they know not what they do" (Luke 23:34). This prayer is a powerful demonstration of Jesus' love and mercy. Even in the midst of His own suffering, He was thinking of the people who were mocking and humiliating Him, asking God to forgive them. This moment reveals the heart of Jesus' mission—He came to save, not to condemn. His response to the humiliation was one of grace and forgiveness, showing that His love for humanity was greater than the pain and shame He was experiencing.

Jesus' humiliation at Calvary also reveals the depth of His humility. In Philippians 2:6-8, we are told that although Jesus was in the very nature God, He did not consider equality with God something to be used to His own advantage. Instead, He made Himself nothing, taking on the form of a servant, and became obedient to death, even death on a cross. Jesus, the Son of God, humbled Himself to the lowest point imaginable. He allowed Himself to be humiliated, mocked, and scorned, even though He had the power to stop it at any moment. This humility is what makes His sacrifice so profound. Jesus did not cling to His divine rights or power; instead, He chose to humble Himself for the sake of humanity. His humiliation was not a sign of weakness, but a demonstration of His incredible strength and love.

At Calvary, Jesus' humiliation was part of the price He paid for our salvation. He endured the shame, the mockery, and the spiritual suffering so that we could be forgiven and reconciled to God. His humiliation was a necessary part of the redemption process—He took on our shame so that we could be set free from it. Because of Jesus' sacrifice, we no longer have to bear the weight of our sins or the shame that comes with them. He bore it all for us at Calvary, and through His humiliation, we are given the gift of grace and forgiveness.

The humiliation of Jesus at Calvary also serves as a powerful example for us as His followers. Jesus taught that those who follow Him must take up their cross and follow Him, and part of this means being willing to endure suffering, humiliation, and rejection for His sake. Jesus' example shows us that true strength is found in humility and that following God's will may sometimes lead to difficult and painful situations. But just as Jesus' humiliation led to victory and redemption, so too can our obedience and humility lead to greater things in God's plan. Jesus' willingness to endure humiliation for the sake of others challenges us to be willing to sacrifice our own pride and comfort for the sake of others and for the sake of the gospel.

In conclusion, Calvary was the place of ultimate humiliation for Jesus Christ, where He was mocked, scorned, and ridiculed by onlookers, yet He endured it all for our sake. His humiliation was not just physical—it was emotional, spiritual, and deeply personal. Jesus was completely innocent, yet He was treated as the worst of criminals, and His body was exposed to shame and suffering. He was mocked for His claims, taunted to save Himself, and ridiculed by those who did not understand the magnitude of what He was doing. Despite this, Jesus did not retaliate or seek to escape the humiliation. Instead, He embraced it as part of God's plan for salvation. His willingness to endure such humiliation shows the depth of His love for humanity and the extent of His humility. At Calvary, Jesus took on the humiliation and shame that we deserved, bearing the weight of the world's sins on His shoulders. Through His humiliation, we are offered the gift of forgiveness and redemption. His response to the mockery and scorn was one of grace, mercy, and forgiveness, revealing the true nature of His mission. Calvary stands as a powerful reminder of the price Jesus paid for our salvation and the incredible love and humility He demonstrated in enduring such humiliation for our sake.

Chapter 18 - Punishment for Sin

The cross was the place where Jesus Christ bore the full punishment for our sins, taking on Himself the weight of all the wrongs humanity has ever committed. This act of sacrifice was not only an immense display of love but also a necessary step to satisfy the wrath of God and provide a way for humanity to be forgiven and reconciled with Him. The Bible tells us in Isaiah 53:6, "All we like sheep have gone astray; we have turned every one to his own way; and the Lord hath laid on him the iniquity of us all." This verse captures the heart of what happened at the cross—every sin, every act of rebellion, and every failure of humanity was placed on Jesus, and He willingly took the punishment that should have been ours. This punishment was the result of God's righteous judgment against sin. Because God is holy and just, He cannot overlook sin. Sin has consequences, and the Bible tells us that the wages of sin is death (Romans 6:23). The cross, therefore, became the place where justice was served, and at the same time, where mercy and grace were extended to all who believe.

To fully grasp the significance of Jesus bearing the punishment for sin, we first need to understand the gravity of sin itself. Sin is any action, thought, or behavior that goes against God's perfect and holy will. It's more than just making mistakes or poor choices—sin is rebellion against God, and it creates a separation between us and Him. From the very beginning, when Adam and Eve disobeyed God in the Garden of Eden, sin entered the world, and with it came death, suffering, and the breakdown of the perfect relationship between humanity and God. Sin is a serious offense because it goes against the very nature of God, who is completely pure, righteous, and just. Every person is guilty of sin because we all fall short of God's perfect standard. The Bible says, "For all have sinned and come short of the glory of God" (Romans 3:23). Because of our sin, we deserve punishment, and that punishment is death—not just physical death, but eternal separation from God.

This is where the cross becomes so important. God, in His love for humanity, did not want us to remain separated from Him. But because He is just, He could not simply ignore our sin. The penalty for sin had to be paid. The cross was God's solution to this problem. Rather than allowing humanity to bear the punishment for their sins, God sent His Son, Jesus, to take our place. Jesus lived a perfect, sinless life, which made Him the only one qualified to bear the punishment for the sins of others. At the cross, Jesus became the substitute for humanity. He took on Himself the full weight of God's wrath against sin, and in doing so, He satisfied the demands of justice. The punishment that was meant for us was placed on Him. This is what theologians call "substitutionary atonement"—Jesus substituted Himself for us, taking the penalty that we deserved.

The punishment that Jesus endured on the cross was both physical and spiritual. The physical suffering that He experienced was beyond anything we can fully comprehend. Before being crucified, Jesus was brutally beaten and scourged. The Roman soldiers used whips embedded with sharp objects that tore into His flesh, leaving Him bleeding and weak. He was mocked, spat upon, and forced to carry His own cross to the place of His execution. Once He arrived at Calvary, nails were driven into His hands and feet, and He was lifted up on the cross to hang until He died. Crucifixion was one of the most painful and humiliating forms of execution, designed to cause maximum suffering. Jesus hung on the cross for hours, struggling to breathe, experiencing excruciating pain with every movement. The physical punishment He endured was horrific, but it was only part of the suffering He bore.

The spiritual suffering that Jesus endured on the cross was even more profound. As He hung there, He was not only experiencing the pain of crucifixion but also bearing the full weight of the world's sins. The Bible tells us that "He himself bore our sins in his body on the tree" (1 Peter 2:24). Every sin that has ever been committed—every lie, every act of violence, every betrayal—was placed on Jesus. He became the embodiment of sin, even though He had never sinned Himself. This is why the Bible says in 2 Corinthians 5:21, "For he hath made him to be sin for us, who knew no sin; that we might be made the righteousness of God in him." Jesus, who was perfectly holy and without sin, took on the guilt and shame of humanity's sins. As He did this, He experienced the separation from God that sin causes. This is why He cried out in agony, "My God, my God, why have you forsaken me?" (Matthew 27:46). In that moment, Jesus was experiencing the full weight of God's wrath against sin. The punishment for sin is separation from God, and Jesus experienced that separation so that we wouldn't have to.

Jesus' willingness to bear the punishment for our sins shows the depth of His love for humanity. He didn't have to endure the cross—He could have called down angels to save Him, but He chose to stay on the cross because He knew it was the only way to save us. In John 10:18, Jesus says, "No man taketh it from me, but I lay it down of myself. I have power to lay it down, and I have power to take it again." His death was not something that happened to Him; it was something He willingly chose to endure. This act of love and obedience to the Father was motivated by His desire to save humanity from the consequences of sin. Jesus knew that without His sacrifice, we would be lost forever, separated from God for eternity. His decision to take on the punishment for our sins was the ultimate act of selflessness and love.

The cross also demonstrates the seriousness of sin. Sometimes people think of sin as something minor or insignificant, but the cross shows us just how serious it really is. Sin is so serious that it required the death of the Son of God to deal with it. The punishment for sin could not be overlooked or minimized. God's justice demanded that the penalty for sin be paid, and Jesus paid that penalty in full. The cross stands as a reminder that sin has real consequences, but it also stands as a symbol of hope because Jesus took those consequences upon Himself. For those who put their faith in Jesus, the punishment for sin has already been paid. We no longer have to fear God's wrath because Jesus has satisfied it on our behalf.

Because Jesus bore the punishment for our sins, we are now offered the gift of forgiveness and eternal life. The Bible tells us that "the wages of sin is death, but the gift of God is eternal life through Jesus Christ our Lord" (Romans 6:23). This gift is not something we can earn or deserve—it is a gift of grace, freely given to us because of what Jesus did on the cross. When we put our faith in Jesus, His sacrifice is applied to us, and we are forgiven of our sins. The punishment that was meant for us has already been paid, and we are no longer under the judgment of sin. Instead, we are declared righteous in God's sight, not because of anything we have done, but because of what Jesus has done for us.

The cross also marks the victory of Jesus over sin and death. When Jesus died on the cross, it may have seemed like a moment of defeat, but in reality, it was the moment of His greatest triumph. By taking on the punishment for sin, Jesus broke the power of sin and death. His death was the final and complete sacrifice for sin, and His resurrection three days later proved that He had defeated death once and for all. Because Jesus conquered death, we have the hope of eternal life. For those who believe in Him, death is not the end—it is the beginning of a new, eternal life with God. The punishment for sin has been dealt with, and death no longer has the final say. Jesus' victory on the cross ensures that we, too, can have victory over sin and death through faith in Him.

In conclusion, the cross was the place where Jesus Christ bore the full punishment for our sins, satisfying the wrath of God and opening the way for humanity to be forgiven and reconciled with God. The punishment that Jesus endured was both physical and spiritual, as He took on the sins of the world and experienced the separation from God that sin causes. His willingness to endure this punishment was an act of incredible love, motivated by His desire to save humanity from the consequences of sin. The cross demonstrates the seriousness of sin and the depth of God's love for us. Through Jesus' sacrifice, the punishment for sin has been paid in full, and we are offered the gift of forgiveness and eternal life. The cross stands as a symbol of both justice and mercy—justice, because the penalty for sin was satisfied, and mercy, because we are now free from that penalty through faith in Jesus. Because of the cross, we no longer have to live in fear of God's wrath; instead, we can live in the freedom and hope that comes from knowing that Jesus has taken our punishment and given us new life. The cross is the ultimate demonstration of God's love and justice, and it is through the cross that we are saved.

Chapter 20 - Propitiation for Sin

At the heart of the Christian faith is the idea that Jesus' sacrifice at Calvary was a propitiation for sin, meaning that through His death, Jesus appeased God's righteous anger and restored peace between God and humanity. This concept is deeply important because it helps us understand why Jesus had to die on the cross and what His death accomplished for the world. In 1 John 2:2, we read, "And he is the propitiation for our sins: and not for ours only, but also for the sins of the whole world." This verse explains that Jesus' sacrifice was not just a random act of love but was specifically aimed at dealing with the problem of sin, which had caused a separation between God and humanity. God is perfectly holy and just, and He cannot overlook sin. Because sin is rebellion against God's will, it brings with it a penalty, and that penalty is death and separation from God. But God, in His love, provided a way for us to be saved from the consequences of our sin, and that way was through the sacrifice of Jesus. Jesus' death on the cross served as a propitiation—a sacrifice that turned away the wrath of God, satisfied His justice, and opened the way for peace between God and man.

To fully appreciate the idea of propitiation, we first need to understand the seriousness of sin and the justice of God. Sin is not just a matter of making mistakes or doing things wrong—it is a fundamental rejection of God's authority and His perfect standards. Sin separates us from God, creating a barrier that we cannot overcome on our own. The Bible tells us that "all have sinned, and come short of the glory of God" (Romans 3:23), which means that every person is guilty of sin and falls short of God's perfect holiness. Sin is not just about breaking rules; it is about breaking the relationship between us and our Creator. Because God is perfectly just, He cannot simply ignore sin or pretend it doesn't matter. Justice requires that sin be punished, and the Bible is clear that the punishment for sin is death: "For the wages of sin is death"

(Romans 6:23). This death is not just physical death, but eternal separation from God, which is the ultimate consequence of sin.

God's anger toward sin is not a reactionary or out-of-control anger. It is a righteous and holy response to everything that goes against His perfect nature. God's wrath is His settled opposition to sin, His rejection of everything that corrupts, destroys, and harms His creation. But while God's justice demands that sin be punished, His love desires that humanity be saved. This creates a tension between God's justice and His mercy—how can a holy and just God forgive sin without compromising His justice? The answer is found in the concept of propitiation, which is what Jesus accomplished through His death on the cross.

When Jesus died on the cross, He took upon Himself the punishment that we deserved for our sins. He became the substitute for us, bearing the wrath of God so that we wouldn't have to. This is what makes Jesus' death a propitiation—it was a sacrifice that turned away God's wrath by satisfying the demands of justice. Jesus' sacrifice was not just about enduring physical pain; it was about taking on the spiritual burden of the world's sins and absorbing the punishment for them. In this way, Jesus' death appeased God's righteous anger against sin. The wrath of God, which should have fallen on us, fell on Jesus instead. He bore the full weight of God's judgment so that we could be spared. This is the essence of propitiation—Jesus stood in our place, took the punishment that was rightfully ours, and through His sacrifice, the wrath of God was satisfied.

One of the most profound aspects of propitiation is that it demonstrates both the justice and the love of God. In His justice, God could not overlook sin or allow it to go unpunished. Sin had to be dealt with, and the punishment had to be carried out. But in His love, God did not want to leave humanity to face the consequences of sin alone. Instead, He provided a way for sin to be punished and for humanity to be forgiven. This way was through the sacrifice of Jesus, who willingly took on Himself the punishment for our sins. In doing so, Jesus satisfied the demands of justice while also demonstrating the incredible love of God. The cross is the place where God's justice and love meet perfectly. On the one hand, the cross shows the seriousness of sin and the reality of God's wrath against it. On the other hand, it shows the depth of God's love, as He was willing to sacrifice His own Son to save us.

Jesus' death as a propitiation also restored peace between God and humanity. Before the cross, sin created a barrier between us and God, making it impossible for us to have a right relationship with Him. Sin separated us from the source of life, love, and peace. But through Jesus' sacrifice, that barrier was removed, and the way was opened for us to be reconciled to God. The Bible tells us that through Jesus, we have peace with God: "Therefore, being justified by faith, we have peace with God through our Lord Jesus Christ" (Romans 5:1). This peace is not just the absence of conflict—it is the restoration of a relationship that had been broken by sin. Because Jesus took the punishment for our sins, we are no longer under the wrath of God. Instead, we are forgiven, and we are welcomed into a relationship with Him. This is the incredible result of propitiation—through Jesus' sacrifice, the enmity between God and humanity is removed, and we are brought into a relationship of peace with God.

Another important aspect of propitiation is that it is universal in scope. In 1 John 2:2, we are told that Jesus is the propitiation for our sins, and not for ours only, but also for the sins of the whole world. This means that Jesus' sacrifice was not just for a select group of people—it was for everyone. His death on the cross provided a way for all people to be forgiven and reconciled to God, no matter who they are or what they have done. The offer of forgiveness and peace with God is extended to all who believe in Jesus. This is the good news of the gospel—through Jesus' death, anyone can be forgiven and brought into a relationship with God. The propitiation that Jesus accomplished is sufficient to cover the sins of the entire world, but it must be personally accepted by each individual through faith in Him.

The idea of propitiation also teaches us about the nature of God's love. The Bible tells us that God loved the world so much that He gave His only Son, that whoever believes in Him should not perish but have eternal life (John 3:16). This love is not a passive or abstract feeling—it is a love that moved God to take action. God's love for humanity is so great that He was willing to sacrifice His own Son to save us from the consequences of our sin. Jesus' death on the cross was the ultimate demonstration of God's love. He did not leave us to face His wrath alone; instead, He provided a way for us to be saved. The cross shows us that God's love is both just and merciful—He dealt with sin in a way that upheld His justice while also extending mercy and grace to humanity. The fact that Jesus was willing to die for us, to take on our punishment, and to restore peace between us and God is a profound expression of His love.

Propitiation also gives us a new perspective on sin and forgiveness. Sometimes people think of sin as a minor issue, something that can be easily forgiven or overlooked. But the cross shows us that sin is serious—it is something that requires the wrath of God to be satisfied. Sin is not just a mistake; it is an offense against a holy God, and it has real consequences. But the cross also shows us that forgiveness is possible, not because we can earn it or deserve it, but because Jesus has already paid the price for our sins. Through His sacrifice, we are offered forgiveness and peace with God. This is the heart of the Christian message: that through Jesus' death, the punishment for sin has been dealt with, and we are invited to receive the gift of forgiveness and eternal life.

The concept of propitiation also reminds us of the importance of faith. While Jesus' sacrifice is sufficient to cover the sins of the whole world, it must be received by faith. The Bible tells us that we are justified by faith in Jesus (Romans 5:1). This means that we must put our trust in Him, believing that His death on the cross was the payment for our sins. Faith is not just intellectual agreement—it is a personal trust in Jesus as our Savior and Lord. When we put our faith in Him, the benefits of His propitiation are applied to us. We are forgiven, we are reconciled to God, and we are brought into a relationship of peace with Him.

In conclusion, Jesus' sacrifice at Calvary was a propitiation for sin, meaning that through His death, He appeased God's righteous anger and restored peace between God and humanity. Sin had created a separation between us and God, and because God is just, sin could not be overlooked. The penalty for sin had to be paid, and Jesus paid that penalty by taking on Himself the full wrath of God. His death satisfied the demands of justice, turning away God's wrath and opening the way for us to be forgiven and reconciled to Him. This act of propitiation demonstrates both the justice and the love of God—He dealt with sin in a way that upheld His holiness, while also extending mercy and grace to humanity. Through Jesus' sacrifice, we are offered peace with God, a restored relationship, and the promise of eternal life. The propitiation that Jesus accomplished is available to all who believe in Him, and it is the foundation of the Christian faith. Because of what Jesus did on the cross, we no longer have to fear God's wrath; instead, we can live in the peace and joy that comes from knowing we are forgiven and loved by God. This is the incredible power of propitiation—Jesus' sacrifice has changed everything, and through Him, we are made right with God.

Chapter 21 - Place of Mockery

At Calvary, Jesus endured unimaginable suffering, not only physically but emotionally and spiritually, as He was mocked and insulted by those around Him during His crucifixion. This mockery came from all sides—soldiers, religious leaders, and even one of the thieves being crucified beside Him. This moment, described in Luke 23:35-39, reveals the depth of human cruelty and the humility with which Jesus endured it all for our sake. The scene at Calvary was not just about the physical agony of the cross; it was also a place of humiliation and mockery, where people ridiculed the very One who had come to save them. The soldiers gambled for His clothes, the religious leaders sneered at Him, and passersby hurled insults, mocking His claims of being the Son of God and challenging Him to save Himself if He truly had the power He had spoken of. Even one of the criminals hanging next to Him joined in the ridicule, saying, "Aren't you the Messiah? Save yourself and us!" (Luke 23:39). In this moment, Jesus faced the ultimate rejection and scorn from the very people He had come to rescue, yet He remained silent, enduring it all out of love and obedience to the Father's plan.

The mockery Jesus endured at Calvary wasn't random—it was deliberate and calculated to wound Him emotionally and psychologically. The soldiers mocked Him by placing a crown of thorns on His head and dressing Him in a purple robe, pretending to bow down and worship Him as "King of the Jews" in a cruel parody of the truth (Mark 15:17-20). They spat on Him, hit Him, and mocked His authority, laughing at the idea that someone like Him could ever be a king. This was not just physical torture; it was an attempt to strip away any dignity He had left. The soldiers didn't understand that they were, in fact, in the presence of the true King, the one who reigns over heaven and earth. Instead, they treated Him as a joke, as though His suffering were something to be amused by. Their mockery was a reflection of humanity's blindness to the truth of who Jesus really is, and it shows the deep misunderstanding and rejection of His mission.

The religious leaders, who had been plotting Jesus' death for some time, also joined in the mockery. These were the men who should have recognized the Messiah when He came, but instead, they rejected Him because He did not fit their expectations of a political or military leader. They saw His crucifixion as a confirmation that He was not the Messiah, and they mocked Him with scornful words, saying, "He saved others; let Him save Himself if He is God's Messiah, the Chosen One" (Luke 23:35). They couldn't see that Jesus was fulfilling His mission in that very moment—that His refusal to come down from the cross was not a sign of weakness, but of the greatest strength. By staying on the cross, Jesus was choosing to complete the work of salvation, even though it meant enduring the insults and humiliation from those who should have honored Him. The religious leaders' mockery shows the tragic irony of the situation—they were mocking the one person who had the power to save them, but they were too blinded by their pride and preconceived ideas to see it.

Even one of the thieves crucified beside Jesus joined in the mockery. This man was dying alongside Jesus, suffering the same fate, yet instead of recognizing Jesus for who He was, he hurled insults at Him, saying, "Aren't you the Messiah? Save yourself and us!" (Luke 23:39). This thief's mockery reflects the same misunderstanding that the religious leaders and soldiers had—he wanted Jesus to prove His power by saving Himself from the cross, not realizing that Jesus' refusal to save Himself was the very act that would make salvation possible for all. The other thief, in contrast, recognized Jesus' innocence and asked to be remembered when Jesus came into His kingdom. This thief's faith in the midst of the mockery around them stands as a powerful contrast, showing that even in the darkest moments, some could see the truth of who Jesus really was. But the mocking thief represents the hardness of heart that so many had toward Jesus, even as He was in the process of offering them the ultimate gift of salvation.

The mockery at Calvary highlights the extent to which Jesus was willing to go to save humanity. He didn't just suffer physically; He endured the emotional and psychological torment of being ridiculed and scorned by the people He loved, the very people He came to save. This mockery was a fulfillment of the prophecy in Isaiah 53:3, which says that the Messiah would be "despised and rejected by men, a man of sorrows, and acquainted with grief." Jesus experienced the full weight of human rejection, yet He did not retaliate or defend Himself. Instead, He remained silent, as Isaiah 53:7 says, "He was oppressed and afflicted, yet He did not open His mouth; He was led like a lamb to the slaughter, and as a sheep before its shearers is silent, so He did not open His mouth." Jesus' silence in the face of mockery was not a sign of weakness; it was a sign of His strength and His commitment to the Father's will. He knew that He had to endure the cross and all the humiliation that came with it in order to accomplish the work of salvation.

The mockery at Calvary also reveals the depths of human sinfulness. The people who mocked Jesus were blind to the truth of who He was, and in their blindness, they rejected the very one who could save them. Their mockery was not just directed at Jesus as a person, but at His mission and identity as the Son of God. By mocking Him, they were rejecting God's plan of salvation, not realizing that in doing so, they were fulfilling it. The religious leaders, the soldiers, and the thief who mocked Jesus were all caught up in their own pride and misunderstanding, and their mockery reflected the hardness of their hearts. They couldn't see that Jesus' suffering was not a sign of defeat, but of victory—victory over sin and death. This blindness to the truth is a powerful reminder of the way sin can distort our understanding and lead us to reject the very things that can save us.

Despite the mockery, Jesus never wavered in His mission. He endured the insults, the laughter, and the scorn with a quiet strength that came from His deep love for humanity. Every insult hurled at Him was another opportunity for Him to demonstrate the depth of His love and commitment to saving the world. Jesus didn't need to prove Himself by coming down from the cross because He knew that the true victory was in staying on it. His refusal to respond to the mockery shows His incredible self-control and His understanding of the bigger picture. He knew that the cross was the means by which salvation would come to humanity, and He was willing to endure the shame and humiliation because of the joy set before Him—the joy of knowing that His sacrifice would make a way for people to be reconciled to God.

The mockery at Calvary also serves as a lesson for us today. It reminds us that following Jesus may sometimes mean enduring ridicule and rejection from the world. Just as Jesus was mocked for His claims to be the Messiah,

Christians may face mockery for their faith in Him. But Jesus' example at Calvary teaches us how to respond—with humility, patience, and love. He didn't lash out at those who mocked Him; instead, He prayed for them, saying, "Father, forgive them, for they do not know what they are doing" (Luke 23:34). This prayer shows the depth of Jesus' compassion, even for those who were actively mocking and insulting Him. It's a reminder that no matter how we are treated, we are called to respond with love and forgiveness, just as Jesus did.

In the end, the mockery at Calvary could not diminish the significance of what Jesus was accomplishing. The people who mocked Him thought they were witnessing the end of His influence, but in reality, they were witnessing the moment that would change history forever. The cross, which seemed like a place of defeat, was actually the place of Jesus' greatest victory—the victory over sin and death. Jesus' willingness to endure the mockery, the pain, and the suffering of the cross is a testament to His incredible love for humanity and His commitment to fulfilling God's plan of salvation. The mockery was painful, but it was also part of the price He was willing to pay to save the world.

In conclusion, Calvary was not only a place of physical suffering for Jesus but also a place of mockery, where He was ridiculed and insulted by soldiers, religious leaders, and even one of the criminals crucified beside Him. This mockery was a reflection of the blindness and hardness of human hearts, as people rejected the very one who had come to save them. Yet, despite the insults and humiliation, Jesus remained silent and endured it all for the sake of humanity. His response to the mockery shows His incredible strength, humility, and love, as He refused to defend Himself or retaliate, knowing that His suffering was necessary to accomplish the work of salvation. The mockery at Calvary reveals the depth of human sinfulness but also the depth of Jesus' love, as He prayed for the forgiveness of those who were mocking Him. In the end, the mockery could not diminish the significance of what Jesus was doing—His sacrifice on the cross was the ultimate act of love and the means by which humanity could be saved. The place of mockery became the place of victory, as Jesus triumphed over sin and death through His willingness to endure the cross.

Chapter 22 - Physical Death

Calvary is the place where Jesus Christ experienced physical death, an event that holds profound meaning not only because of its historical significance but because of its spiritual impact on humanity. Jesus' physical death on the cross was not just the tragic end of a life—it was the pivotal moment in God's plan to bring salvation to the world. In 1 Peter 3:18, we read, "For Christ also hath once suffered for sins, the just for the unjust, that he might bring us to God, being put to death in the flesh, but quickened by the Spirit." This verse summarizes the importance of Jesus' death: He, the sinless and righteous one, died in the flesh to bring spiritual life to all who believe in Him. His physical death was the ultimate sacrifice, necessary to pay the price for humanity's sins and to restore the broken relationship between God and mankind. In dying, Jesus took upon Himself the punishment that was meant for us, allowing us the opportunity to be reconciled to God and receive the gift of eternal life.

The physical death of Jesus at Calvary is central to the Christian faith because it addresses the most serious problem facing humanity: sin and its consequences. Sin, which entered the world through the disobedience of Adam and Eve, separates humanity from God. It corrupts our nature, leads to brokenness in our relationships, and ultimately results in death—both physical and spiritual. The Bible teaches that "the wages of sin is death" (Romans 6:23), meaning that death is the natural consequence of sin. Sin creates a chasm between us and God, and no matter how hard we try, we cannot bridge that gap on our own. The physical death of Jesus on the cross was God's solution to this problem. Because Jesus was without sin, He was the only one qualified to take on the penalty for the sins of the world. His death was not an ordinary death—it was a sacrificial death, offered willingly to satisfy the demands of God's justice and to bring salvation to humanity.

The suffering that Jesus endured leading up to His physical death was immense. Before being nailed to the cross, He was subjected to brutal flogging, a punishment so severe that it left Him bloodied and weakened. Roman soldiers mocked Him, placing a crown of thorns on His head and striking Him repeatedly. He was forced to carry His own cross through the streets of Jerusalem to the place of His crucifixion, a journey that was made all the more painful by the physical abuse He had already endured. When He arrived at Calvary, nails were driven through His hands and feet, and He was hoisted up on the cross to hang between two criminals. Crucifixion was one of the most excruciating forms of execution, designed to prolong the victim's suffering as they slowly died from a combination of blood loss, dehydration, and asphyxiation. Jesus' physical death on the cross was not quick or easy—it was agonizing and humiliating, a public display of brutality meant to shame and degrade Him. Yet, despite the intense physical suffering, Jesus willingly endured it, knowing that His death was necessary for the salvation of humanity.

Jesus' physical death was not only about enduring pain—it was about accomplishing a divine purpose. Throughout His life, Jesus made it clear that He had come to do the will of His Father, and that His ultimate mission was to lay down His life for the sins of the world. In John 10:17-18, Jesus said, "Therefore doth my Father love me, because I lay down my life, that I might take it again. No man taketh it from me, but I lay it down of myself. I have power to lay it down, and I have power to take it again." Jesus' death was not a result of circumstances spiraling out of control—it was a deliberate and voluntary act of obedience to the Father's will. He chose to go to the cross, knowing that it was the only way to provide salvation for humanity. His physical death was the fulfillment of centuries of prophecy and the culmination of God's plan to redeem the world.

One of the most remarkable aspects of Jesus' physical death is that it was not the end of the story. His death was the gateway to something far greater—His resurrection and the promise of new life for all who believe in Him. The Bible teaches that through His death and resurrection, Jesus conquered sin and death, opening the way for humanity to be reconciled to God. In 1 Corinthians 15:21-22, Paul writes, "For since by man came death, by man came also the resurrection of the dead. For as in Adam all die, even so in Christ shall all be made alive." Jesus' physical death was the means by which He overcame the power of death, not just for Himself, but for all who trust in Him. Because of His death, we have the hope of eternal life—a life that transcends the physical death we all must face.

Jesus' physical death at Calvary also highlights the depth of God's love for humanity. The cross is the ultimate demonstration of God's love, a love so profound that He was willing to sacrifice His own Son to save us. In John 3:16, one of the most famous verses in the Bible, we read, "For God so loved the world that he gave his only begotten Son, that whosoever believeth in him should not perish, but have everlasting life." This verse captures the heart of the gospel message—God's love for us is so great that He was willing to give up His Son to experience physical death on our behalf. Jesus did not have to die; He chose to die out of love for us, knowing that His death was the only way to reconcile us to God. His willingness to endure the physical suffering and death of the cross is a testament to the lengths God will go to save those He loves.

The physical death of Jesus also serves as a model for us as His followers. Jesus taught that those who wish to follow Him must take up their own cross, deny themselves, and follow Him (Matthew 16:24). While we are not called to physically die in the same way that Jesus did, we are called to die to ourselves—to lay down our own desires, ambitions, and sinful tendencies in order to follow the will of God. Jesus' physical death on the cross was an act of ultimate self-sacrifice, and we are called to follow His example by living lives of selflessness, love, and obedience to God. The cross reminds us that following Jesus often involves sacrifice, but it also brings the promise of new life—both in this world and in the life to come.

Another important aspect of Jesus' physical death is its significance in fulfilling the requirements of the Old Testament sacrificial system. In the Jewish tradition, animal sacrifices were required as a temporary covering for sin. These sacrifices were a symbol of the need for atonement, but they were not sufficient to fully remove the guilt of sin. The blood of animals could never completely take away sin—it only pointed to the need for a greater, perfect sacrifice. Jesus' death on the cross was that perfect sacrifice. As the spotless Lamb of God, His death fully satisfied the requirements of God's justice and provided a permanent solution to the problem of sin. Hebrews 9:12-14 explains, "Neither by the blood of goats and calves, but by his own blood he entered in once into the holy place, having obtained eternal redemption for us. For if the blood of bulls and of goats, and the ashes of an heifer sprinkling the unclean, sanctifieth to the purifying of the flesh: how much more shall the blood of Christ, who through the eternal Spirit offered himself without spot to God, purge your conscience from dead works to serve the living God?" Jesus' physical death on the cross accomplished what the Old Testament sacrifices could never do—it provided a once-for-all atonement for sin, making it possible for humanity to be forgiven and cleansed.

Calvary is also the place where the power of sin was broken. Before Jesus' death, sin had a strong grip on humanity, causing people to live in spiritual darkness and separation from God. But through His death, Jesus broke the power of sin, setting humanity free from its bondage. In Romans 6:6, Paul writes, "Knowing this, that our old man is crucified with him, that the body of sin might be destroyed, that henceforth we should not serve sin." Jesus' death was not just about paying the penalty for sin—it was about breaking the power of sin over our lives. Because of His death, we are no longer slaves to sin. We are free to live in the newness of life that Jesus offers, no longer bound by the sinful nature that once controlled us.

In conclusion, Calvary is where Jesus experienced physical death, dying in the flesh so that He might bring us spiritual life. His death was not an ordinary death—it was the ultimate sacrifice, offered willingly to pay the penalty for the sins of humanity. Through His death, Jesus took upon Himself the punishment that was meant for us, satisfying the demands of God's justice and opening the way for us to be reconciled to God. His physical death was the fulfillment of God's plan of salvation, and it was the means by which He overcame the power of sin and death. The cross is a symbol of both suffering and victory, as Jesus' death was the gateway to His resurrection and the promise of new life for all who believe in Him. Jesus' physical death at Calvary is the ultimate demonstration of God's love for humanity, and it serves as a model for how we are called to live lives of self-sacrifice, love, and obedience. Because of His death, we have the hope of eternal life, the forgiveness of sins, and the freedom to live in the power of His resurrection.

Chapter 23 - Place of Two Thieves

At Calvary, Jesus was crucified between two thieves, an event rich with symbolism that emphasizes the choice every person must make: to accept or reject Him. This powerful scene is captured in Luke 23:39-43, where we see two very different reactions to Jesus as He hung on the cross. One thief mocked Jesus, saying, "Aren't you the Messiah? Save yourself and us!" (Luke 23:39). This thief represents those who reject Jesus, those who fail to understand His true purpose and instead ridicule or dismiss Him. He was only concerned with his own suffering and demanded that Jesus use His power to provide an immediate escape from death. His words reveal a heart hardened by disbelief and bitterness, unable or unwilling to see that Jesus was not there to save Himself, but to save humanity. In contrast, the other thief rebuked the first, saying, "Don't you fear God, since you are under the same sentence? We are punished justly, for we are getting what our deeds deserve. But this man has done nothing wrong" (Luke 23:40-41). This second thief acknowledged his own guilt and recognized Jesus' innocence. In a moment of faith, he turned to Jesus and said, "Jesus, remember me when you come into your kingdom" (Luke 23:42). Jesus' response to this repentant thief was remarkable: "Truly I tell you, today you will be with me in paradise" (Luke 23:43). In this brief exchange, we see the core of the gospel message—salvation comes to those who repent, believe, and put their trust in Jesus.

The two thieves on either side of Jesus symbolize the two responses that people have toward Him. Every person is faced with a decision, just like these two men. We can either reject Jesus, as the first thief did, or we can accept Him, like the second thief. This choice is the most important decision anyone can make because it determines not only how we live our lives but also where we will spend eternity. The first thief, in his mocking and disbelief, represents the people who turn away from Jesus, who question or reject His power to save.

His attitude is one of pride and cynicism, thinking only of immediate physical relief rather than recognizing his deeper spiritual need. He failed to see that the true salvation Jesus was offering wasn't from the temporary suffering of the cross, but from the eternal consequences of sin. This thief, in his rejection of Jesus, missed the opportunity for redemption and forgiveness. His mocking words are reflective of a heart closed to the grace of God, focusing only on the here and now, blinded by the pain of the moment and unable to see the bigger picture of salvation that was unfolding before him.

On the other hand, the second thief represents those who, in their moment of desperation, recognize their need for a Savior and turn to Jesus in faith. This man, though a criminal, had the humility to admit his guilt and acknowledge that he deserved the punishment he was receiving. He didn't ask Jesus to take him down from the cross or to save him from physical death. Instead, he asked to be remembered in Jesus' kingdom, showing that he understood something deeper about who Jesus was. In his dying moments, this thief expressed faith in Jesus' power and authority, despite the fact that Jesus was suffering alongside him. His faith was remarkable because, from a human perspective, it didn't look like Jesus had any power at all. Jesus was hanging on a cross, beaten, bloodied, and dying. But the second thief saw beyond the physical appearance and recognized that Jesus was indeed the Messiah, the King, and that His kingdom was not of this world. His request, "Remember me when you come into your kingdom," was a declaration of faith in Jesus' ability to save, even as He hung on the cross.

Jesus' response to the second thief is one of the most beautiful promises in Scripture. He didn't rebuke the thief for his past sins or tell him it was too late. Instead, He assured him that "today you will be with me in paradise." This is the essence of grace—undeserved, unearned, and freely given. The thief didn't have time to make up for his sins, to do good works, or to change his life. He was at the end of his life, with nothing to offer but faith in Jesus. And that was enough. Jesus' words to him demonstrate that salvation is not based on what we do, but on our faith in Him. The thief's past didn't disqualify him from receiving God's grace, just as our past doesn't disqualify us. The thief's simple act of faith, his recognition of who Jesus was, was enough to secure his place in paradise. This moment at Calvary is a powerful reminder that no one is beyond the reach of

God's grace, no matter how far they've fallen or how late in life they come to faith.

The two thieves also represent the contrast between human pride and humility. The first thief, in his arrogance, couldn't see past his own suffering and mocked Jesus, demanding that He prove His power by saving them from the cross. This attitude reflects the pride that often prevents people from coming to Jesus. Many people today, like the first thief, are unwilling to humble themselves and admit their need for a Savior. They refuse to believe in Jesus unless He meets their demands or expectations. They want Him to fix their immediate problems without recognizing that their greatest need is spiritual. The second thief, however, demonstrated humility. He admitted his guilt and acknowledged that he deserved the punishment he was receiving. He didn't demand anything from Jesus; he simply asked to be remembered. This humility is what opened the door for him to receive Jesus' grace. It's a reminder that salvation begins with humility—with recognizing that we are sinners in need of a Savior and that we cannot save ourselves.

The scene at Calvary, with Jesus between the two thieves, also illustrates the inclusivity of the gospel. Jesus' offer of salvation is for everyone, regardless of their past. The second thief had lived a life of crime, yet in his final moments, he found forgiveness and eternal life. This shows us that it's never too late to turn to Jesus, no matter what we've done. The grace of God is available to anyone who will humble themselves and put their faith in Jesus. The second thief's story is one of hope for all of us. It reminds us that no one is beyond redemption, and that even in our darkest moments, Jesus is there, offering us the gift of salvation if we will only accept it.

This moment at Calvary also serves as a warning to those who, like the first thief, reject Jesus. The first thief had the same opportunity as the second thief. He was in the same position, facing the same fate, and he was just as close to Jesus. But instead of turning to Jesus in faith, he mocked Him. This shows us that proximity to Jesus is not enough. Being near Jesus, hearing about Him, or even witnessing His power doesn't guarantee salvation. Each person must make a personal decision to accept or reject Jesus. The first thief chose to reject Him, and as a result, he missed out on the grace and forgiveness that Jesus was offering, even in that moment. This is a sobering reminder that the decision to accept or reject Jesus is one that every person must make for themselves, and it has eternal consequences.

The crucifixion of Jesus between the two thieves also highlights the paradox of the cross. From a worldly perspective, Jesus hanging on the cross between two criminals looked like a defeat. It appeared as though Jesus was powerless, defeated, and humiliated. But in reality, this was the moment of His greatest victory. By staying on the cross, Jesus was accomplishing the work of salvation. He could have come down from the cross, as the first thief mocked Him to do, but He chose to remain because He knew that His death was the only way to save humanity. The cross, which looked like a place of shame and defeat, was actually the place where Jesus won the victory over sin and death. The second thief, in his moment of faith, recognized this, and because of that, he was promised eternal life. The first thief, blinded by his pride and disbelief, could only see the suffering and the seeming defeat. This contrast reminds us that faith often requires us to see beyond the surface, to trust in God's plan even when it doesn't make sense from a human perspective.

In conclusion, the scene of Jesus crucified between two thieves at Calvary symbolizes the choice that every person must make: to accept or reject Him. The first thief, in his pride and disbelief, mocked Jesus and demanded that He save Himself. He represents those who reject Jesus, refusing to humble themselves and recognize their need for a Savior. The second thief, however, in a moment of humility and faith, acknowledged his guilt and asked Jesus to remember him in His kingdom. His faith, even in the final moments of his life, secured his place in paradise. This scene at Calvary is a powerful reminder of the grace of God, available to all who will humble themselves and put their trust in Jesus. It shows us that no one is beyond redemption and that it's never too late to turn to Jesus. At the same time, it serves as a warning that rejecting Jesus has eternal consequences. The two thieves represent the two paths before every person—faith or rejection, life or death. The choice is ours to make, and it's a choice that carries eternal significance.

Chapter 24 - Proclamation of Salvation

At Calvary, one of the most profound moments in all of history took place when Jesus, hanging on the cross, proclaimed His final words, "It is finished" (John 19:30). These words are more than just a declaration of the end of His earthly life; they are the proclamation of salvation and the completion of His redemptive work. In this single, powerful statement, Jesus was announcing that everything He had come to accomplish—God's plan to save humanity from sin—was fulfilled. "It is finished" meant that the work of salvation was done, the debt of sin was paid in full, and the way for humanity to be reconciled with God was now open. This moment at Calvary marked the climax of Jesus' mission, where His sacrifice on the cross completed the work that had been planned by God since the beginning of time. It was the culmination of Jesus' life of perfect obedience, His fulfillment of the Old Testament prophecies, and the ultimate act of love that would change the course of history forever.

When Jesus said, "It is finished," He was speaking about the completion of His purpose on earth—the purpose of bringing salvation to humanity. From the moment sin entered the world through Adam and Eve, there had been a separation between God and humanity. Sin created a barrier that no amount of human effort could overcome. God, in His holiness and justice, could not simply ignore sin; it had to be dealt with. The penalty for sin was death and eternal separation from God. But because of God's great love for humanity, He made a way for us to be saved from the consequences of sin. This way was through the life, death, and resurrection of Jesus Christ. Jesus came into the world to live a sinless life, to fulfill the requirements of the law, and to be the perfect sacrifice for the sins of the world. When He said, "It is finished," He was declaring that this work was complete—that the debt of sin had been paid in full by His death on the cross. No further sacrifices would ever be needed, no additional work was required. Jesus' death was the final and complete payment for sin.

The phrase "It is finished" is also deeply connected to the concept of atonement. In the Old Testament, the Israelites had to offer animal sacrifices to atone for their sins. These sacrifices were a temporary covering for sin, but they could never fully take it away. The blood of animals could not truly cleanse the guilt of sin; it was only a shadow of the greater sacrifice that was to come. Jesus was the fulfillment of those sacrificial systems. He was the Lamb of God, the perfect and sinless sacrifice, whose death would atone for the sins of the world once and for all. When He declared, "It is finished," He was announcing that the system of sacrifices was no longer necessary because He had fulfilled the ultimate sacrifice. His blood, shed on the cross, was enough to cleanse humanity from all sin, past, present, and future. The atonement was complete, and through His sacrifice, we are made right with God.

This proclamation of salvation also signified the defeat of sin, death, and Satan. Before Jesus' death, sin had power over humanity, leading to spiritual death and separation from God. But by dying on the cross, Jesus broke the power of sin. His death paid the penalty for sin, and His resurrection three days later demonstrated His victory over death. Death no longer had the final say. Jesus' sacrifice defeated the power of Satan, the one who had held humanity in bondage through sin. In His death, Jesus disarmed the powers and authorities, making a public spectacle of them, triumphing over them by the cross (Colossians 2:15). When Jesus said, "It is finished," He was proclaiming that the forces of evil had been defeated and that salvation had been won. Through His death, Jesus conquered sin and death, and He opened the way for eternal life for all who believe in Him. This victory is not just for a select few; it is available to everyone who puts their faith in Jesus and accepts His gift of salvation.

The phrase "It is finished" also carries the meaning of a task being completed perfectly. Jesus' life and mission were carried out in perfect obedience to the Father's will. From the moment of His birth to His death on the cross, Jesus lived a life of sinless perfection, fulfilling every requirement of God's law. He resisted every temptation, lived in perfect righteousness, and did everything that the Father had sent Him to do. His death on the cross was the final act of obedience, the culmination of a life lived in perfect submission to

God's plan. When He said, "It is finished," He was announcing that He had done everything that needed to be done to accomplish our salvation. There was nothing left undone, no part of God's plan that was incomplete. Jesus had fulfilled every prophecy, every law, and every promise. His work was perfect, and because of that, our salvation is secure.

Jesus' proclamation at Calvary is also an invitation to all people to enter into the salvation He has provided. By saying "It is finished," Jesus was declaring that the work of redemption is complete, but it is up to each person to accept that gift. The door to salvation has been opened, but we must choose to walk through it. Jesus' death on the cross made it possible for us to be forgiven of our sins and to be reconciled with God, but we must put our faith in Him to receive that forgiveness. The proclamation of salvation at Calvary is a message of hope for all humanity. It is the good news that, no matter who we are or what we have done, Jesus has paid the price for our sins, and we can be forgiven. His work is finished, and now the offer of salvation is extended to everyone who will believe in Him.

"It is finished" also means that there is nothing we can add to what Jesus has already done. Salvation is not something we can earn through our own efforts or good works. Jesus' death on the cross was sufficient to pay the full price for our sins. No amount of religious activity, moral behavior, or charitable deeds can add to what Jesus has already accomplished. Our salvation is a gift, freely given by God through the sacrifice of His Son. All we need to do is accept that gift by putting our faith in Jesus. When we trust in Him, we are forgiven, and we receive the gift of eternal life. The work is done, the price is paid, and the door to heaven is open because of what Jesus did at Calvary. This is the essence of grace—undeserved, unearned, and freely given.

The proclamation of salvation at Calvary also marked the fulfillment of God's promises throughout Scripture. From the moment sin entered the world, God promised that He would one day send a Savior to crush the power of sin and restore humanity's relationship with Him. Throughout the Old Testament, prophets foretold the coming of the Messiah, the one who would bear the sins of the world and bring salvation. Jesus was the fulfillment of those promises. His life, death, and resurrection were the realization of everything God had been pointing toward throughout history. When Jesus said, "It is finished," He was declaring that God's plan of salvation, which had been in motion since the beginning of time, was now complete. Every promise had been fulfilled, every prophecy had come true, and the way of salvation was now open to all who would believe. This shows us the faithfulness of God—He always keeps His promises, and through Jesus, He has provided a way for us to be saved.

Jesus' proclamation of salvation at Calvary is also a message of victory. His death on the cross may have looked like defeat to those who were watching, but in reality, it was the greatest victory in history. Through His death, Jesus defeated the power of sin, death, and Satan. He won the victory over every force of evil that had held humanity in bondage. When He said, "It is finished," He was declaring that the battle had been won. The forces of darkness had been defeated, and the way of salvation was now open. This victory is not just for Jesus—it is a victory that we share in when we put our faith in Him. Because Jesus won the victory over sin and death, we too can have victory over sin and death. We no longer have to live in fear of death, because Jesus has opened the way to eternal life. We no longer have to be slaves to sin, because Jesus has set us free. His victory is our victory, and it is a victory that lasts for all eternity.

In conclusion, Jesus' final words at Calvary, "It is finished," are the proclamation of salvation and the completion of His redemptive work. These words declare that the work of salvation is done, the debt of sin is paid in full, and the way to eternal life is open to all who will believe in Him. Jesus' death on the cross was the perfect and final sacrifice for sin, fulfilling the requirements of God's law and satisfying His justice. It was the fulfillment of God's promises throughout Scripture and the ultimate demonstration of His love for humanity. Through His death, Jesus won the victory over sin, death, and Satan, and He opened the way for us to be forgiven and reconciled to God. His proclamation, "It is finished," is a message of hope, grace, and victory, reminding us that there is nothing we can add to what Jesus has already done. Salvation is a gift, freely given, and all we need to do is accept it by putting our faith in Him. The work is done, the price is paid, and the door to eternal life is open because of what Jesus accomplished at Calvary.

Chapter 25 - Permanent Atonement

The sacrifice that Jesus made at Calvary was the most significant event in all of history because it provided a permanent atonement for sin, a once-for-all sacrifice that was sufficient to cover the sins of all who believe, for all time. This act of atonement, which we read about in Hebrews 10:10, declares that through Jesus' death on the cross, "we have been sanctified through the offering of the body of Jesus Christ once for all." These words tell us that the sacrifice Jesus made at Calvary was not just a temporary fix or a partial solution; it was a complete and final payment for sin that never needs to be repeated. Unlike the sacrifices in the Old Testament, which had to be offered again and again because they could never fully remove sin, Jesus' sacrifice was perfect and sufficient. His death covered the sins of the past, present, and future, offering salvation to everyone who would put their faith in Him. The significance of this permanent atonement is that it changes everything about how we relate to God and how we understand forgiveness, grace, and the possibility of eternal life.

In the Old Testament, the people of Israel were required to offer animal sacrifices as a way of temporarily atoning for their sins. The blood of bulls, goats, and lambs was shed to symbolize the payment for sin, but these sacrifices had to be repeated over and over again because they could never fully remove the guilt of sin. Hebrews 10:4 explains that "it is impossible for the blood of bulls and goats to take away sins." These sacrifices were merely a shadow of the greater sacrifice that was to come—Jesus Christ, the Lamb of God, who would take away the sins of the world. The temporary nature of the Old Testament sacrifices highlighted the fact that a more perfect sacrifice was needed, one that could provide a permanent solution to the problem of sin. That perfect sacrifice was made when Jesus, the Son of God, willingly laid down His life at Calvary. His sacrifice was different from the animal sacrifices of the Old Testament because it was final and complete. When Jesus died on the cross, He declared, "It is finished" (John 19:30), signifying that the work of atonement was done. There would be no need for any more sacrifices because His death fully satisfied the requirements of God's justice.

The concept of atonement means that Jesus took our place on the cross, bearing the punishment that we deserved for our sins. Sin separates us from God, and because God is holy and just, He cannot ignore or overlook sin. Sin requires a penalty, and that penalty is death—both physical death and eternal separation from God. But because of His great love for us, God provided a way for our sins to be forgiven without compromising His justice. That way was through the sacrifice of His Son, Jesus. Jesus lived a sinless life, which made Him the only one qualified to take on the sins of the world. When He died on the cross, He took upon Himself the punishment that was meant for us, offering His life as a substitute for ours. His death was the ultimate act of love and obedience, and it accomplished what no other sacrifice could—permanent atonement for sin. This means that anyone who puts their faith in Jesus can be forgiven and reconciled to God because the price for their sin has already been paid in full.

The permanent nature of Jesus' sacrifice is one of the most important aspects of the gospel. In Hebrews 10:11-12, we read, "Day after day every priest stands and performs his religious duties; again and again he offers the same sacrifices, which can never take away sins. But when this priest [Jesus] had offered for all time one sacrifice for sins, he sat down at the right hand of God." This passage contrasts the repetitive nature of the Old Testament sacrifices with the finality of Jesus' sacrifice. The fact that Jesus "sat down" at the right hand of God after offering His sacrifice is significant because it indicates that His work was complete. In the temple, the priests never sat down because their work was never finished—they had to keep offering sacrifices. But Jesus' sacrifice was different; it was once for all. There was no need for any further sacrifices because His death fully accomplished the forgiveness of sins.

This permanent atonement also means that there is nothing we can add to what Jesus has already done. Our salvation is not based on our own efforts or good works; it is entirely based on the sacrifice that Jesus made at Calvary. This is why salvation is often described as a gift—it is something that we receive, not something that we earn. Ephesians 2:8-9 says, "For it is by grace you have been saved, through faith—and this is not from yourselves, it is the gift of God—not by works, so that no one can boast." The fact that Jesus' sacrifice is sufficient for all time means that we don't have to try to earn God's favor through our own actions. We simply need to trust in what Jesus has already done for us. His sacrifice was enough, and because of that, we can rest in the assurance that our sins are forgiven.

The permanence of Jesus' atonement also brings tremendous peace and security to those who believe in Him. Because His sacrifice was complete, we don't have to live in fear of whether we have done enough to be saved. The work of salvation was finished at the cross, and when we put our faith in Jesus, we are fully and forever forgiven. Hebrews 10:14 says, "For by one sacrifice he has made perfect forever those who are being made holy." This means that our standing before God is not based on our own righteousness but on the righteousness of Jesus, which has been credited to us through His sacrifice. This gives us confidence and assurance in our relationship with God. We don't have to live in fear of judgment because Jesus has already taken the judgment for us. We are accepted by God not because of what we have done but because of what Jesus has done.

The once-for-all nature of Jesus' sacrifice also highlights the depth of God's love for humanity. The fact that Jesus was willing to suffer and die on the cross to provide permanent atonement for our sins is a testament to how much God loves us. In Romans 5:8, we read, "But God demonstrates his own love for us in this: While we were still sinners, Christ died for us." Jesus didn't wait for us to clean up our lives or become worthy of His sacrifice. He died for us while we were still sinners, offering Himself as the perfect sacrifice so that we could be forgiven and reconciled to God. His sacrifice was motivated by love—love for the world and love for each one of us individually. The permanence of His atonement shows that His love is not conditional or temporary; it is eternal. Once we put our faith in Jesus, we are forever secure in His love, knowing that nothing can separate us from it.

Jesus' sacrifice at Calvary was also sufficient to cover the sins of the whole world. The atonement He provided is not limited to a specific group of people; it is available to everyone who believes in Him. In 1 John 2:2, we read, "He is the atoning sacrifice for our sins, and not only for ours but also for the sins of the whole world." This means that no one is beyond the reach of God's grace. No matter what we have done or how far we have fallen, Jesus' sacrifice is enough to cover our sins. The offer of forgiveness and eternal life is open to all who will put their trust in Him. This is the good news of the gospel—that through Jesus, anyone can be forgiven, and anyone can be saved.

The permanent atonement provided by Jesus also changes the way we live. When we truly understand what Jesus has done for us, it transforms our hearts and our lives. We no longer live under the burden of guilt and shame because we know that our sins have been forgiven. We no longer strive to earn God's approval because we know that we are already accepted through Jesus. This frees us to live lives of gratitude, love, and obedience, not out of fear or obligation, but out of a deep sense of thankfulness for what Jesus has done. The atonement Jesus provided at Calvary gives us a new identity—we are no longer defined by our sins or failures but by the righteousness of Jesus. We are children of God, forgiven and loved, and that changes everything about how we live.

In conclusion, the sacrifice that Jesus made at Calvary was a once-for-all atonement, sufficient to cover the sins of all who believe, for all time. His death on the cross was the perfect and final payment for sin, fully satisfying the requirements of God's justice and providing a way for humanity to be forgiven and reconciled to God. Unlike the sacrifices in the Old Testament, which had to be repeated over and over again, Jesus' sacrifice was complete and permanent. It never needs to be repeated because it accomplished everything that was necessary for our salvation. This permanent atonement brings peace and security to those who believe, knowing that their sins are forgiven and that they are forever accepted by God. It also demonstrates the depth of God's love for us, as Jesus willingly laid down His life to provide the way of salvation. The offer of forgiveness and eternal life is open to everyone, and it is based entirely on what Jesus has done, not on anything we can do. The once-for-all nature of Jesus' sacrifice frees us from the burden of trying to earn God's favor and allows us to live in the joy and freedom of knowing that we are loved, forgiven, and secure in Him forever.

Conclusion

As we conclude "Reflections on Calvary's Cross," we are reminded that the cross is not just a moment in history but a call to live each day in light of the incredible sacrifice Jesus made for us. The cross is the foundation of our faith and the place where our journey with the Lord truly begins. But it's more than that—it's the compass that guides us in how we are to live every single day. The cross shows us the depth of God's love, and as Christians, we are called to respond to that love by walking with Him faithfully, humbly, and gratefully. The journey doesn't end at Calvary; in fact, it's where our new life begins. To walk with the Lord means to carry the lessons of the cross in our hearts every day, allowing the sacrifice of Jesus to shape how we live, how we love, and how we serve others. Jesus' death on the cross was not just for our salvation but also an invitation to live a life transformed by His grace, reflecting His love in everything we do.

As Christians, continuing in our walk with the Lord means living a life that is centered on the cross. The cross reminds us of our own sin and the grace we've been given, and that should humble us daily. We must never forget the price that was paid for our redemption. Walking with the Lord means we continually return to the cross, remembering that it was there that our sins were forgiven, and because of that, we are now free to live in a way that honors God. Our walk with Jesus is not about trying to earn His love or prove our worth—He has already shown us our worth on the cross. It's about living in response to what He has done for us. It's about surrendering our lives to Him, just as He surrendered His life for us. The cross is our reminder that we are called to die to ourselves, to lay down our selfish desires, and to live for Christ. As the Apostle Paul wrote, "I have been crucified with Christ and I no longer live, but Christ lives in me" (Galatians 2:20). This is the heart of the Christian life—to live in such a way that it is Christ who is seen in us.

Continuing in our walk with the Lord also means carrying the love of the cross into the world. Jesus didn't die just so that we could be forgiven; He died to transform us into people who reflect His love to others. The love that Jesus showed on the cross—selfless, sacrificial, and unconditional—is the same love we are called to show to the world. As we reflect on the cross, we are reminded that we are now ambassadors of Christ, called to live out the gospel in our words and actions. This means forgiving others as we have been forgiven, loving others even when it's hard, and serving others with the same humility that Jesus demonstrated. The cross teaches us that true greatness comes from serving others, just as Jesus, the King of Kings, became a servant for our sake. To walk with the Lord is to follow in His footsteps, to love as He loved, and to serve as He served.

But walking with the Lord is not always easy. The Christian life is often marked by trials, challenges, and sacrifices. Yet, the cross reminds us that we are not alone. Jesus understands our struggles because He suffered for us. When we face hardships, we can look to the cross and remember that Jesus endured the ultimate suffering so that we could have the strength to persevere. The cross is a symbol of hope, reminding us that even in our darkest moments, God is with us, and His love will carry us through. As we walk with the Lord, we are called to trust in Him, even when the path is difficult, knowing that the same power that raised Jesus from the dead is at work in us. The cross gives us the confidence to press on, knowing that our victory is secure in Christ.

Continuing in our walk with the Lord also means growing in our relationship with Him. The cross invites us into a deeper intimacy with God. Through Jesus' sacrifice, the barrier of sin has been removed, and we now have direct access to God. Walking with the Lord means spending time in His presence, seeking Him in prayer, and listening to His voice through His Word. It means allowing His Spirit to lead and guide us each day. The more we reflect on the cross, the more we are reminded of God's incredible love for us, and that love should draw us closer to Him. Walking with the Lord is about cultivating a relationship with Him, knowing that He is not just our Savior but our constant companion, our friend, and our guide. The cross is the ultimate expression of God's desire to be with us, and as we walk with Him, we are invited to experience the fullness of His love and grace.

As we continue in our walk with the Lord, we must also remember that the cross is a symbol of victory. Jesus' death was not the end of the story—His resurrection proved that death has been defeated and that we have been given new life in Him. Walking with the Lord means living in the reality of that victory. We no longer walk in fear or defeat because we know that Jesus has already won the battle. The cross reminds us that we are more than conquerors through Him who loved us (Romans 8:37). As we face the challenges of life, we can walk with confidence, knowing that the same power that raised Jesus from the dead is alive in us. The cross is not just a reminder of what Jesus did for us in the past; it's a reminder of the power we have in the present and the hope we have for the future.

The cross is the starting point, but it is also the guidepost that directs us each day. It calls us to live lives of humility, love, and service, always remembering the price that was paid for our salvation. Walking with the Lord means living in the shadow of the cross, allowing its truth to shape who we are and how we live. It means trusting in His grace, resting in His love, and following His example. The cross is a reminder that we are forgiven, redeemed, and loved beyond measure, and as we continue in our walk with the Lord, may we never lose sight of the incredible gift that was given to us at Calvary. May the cross be our constant reminder of God's love, our source of strength, and the foundation of our faith as we journey through this life with Him.

Don't miss out!

Visit the website below and you can sign up to receive emails whenever Joshua Rhoades publishes a new book. There's no charge and no obligation.

https://books2read.com/r/B-A-AJLBB-BHNCF

BOOKS 2 READ

Connecting independent readers to independent writers.

Did you love *Reflections on Calvary's Cross*? Then you should read *Answer The Call - 31 Days of Biblical Action*[1] by Joshua Rhoades!

[2]

"Answer the Call – 31 Days of Biblical Action" is a transformative devotional that challenges you to not only read the Word of God but to live it every day. This powerful 31-day guide is uniquely centered around individual action verbs drawn from Scripture, calling you to apply specific actions in your daily life. Each day highlights a verb—such as love, serve, forgive, trust, or pray—and encourages you to engage deeply with its biblical meaning while putting it into practice.

This is not just a devotional for reflection; it's a call to action, a stirring reminder that faith is most alive when it moves. By focusing on one verb each day, "Answer the Call" helps you to integrate the teachings of the Bible into your daily routine, bringing the message of Scripture to life in practical and meaningful ways.

---

1. https://books2read.com/u/4X5kG9

2. https://books2read.com/u/4X5kG9

The book invites you to engage your heart and hands as you follow Christ's example. Each action verb acts as a catalyst for spiritual growth, reminding you that faith isn't static but dynamic and responsive. Whether it's through acts of kindness, moments of prayer, or stepping out in faith, these daily challenges will inspire you to live out your beliefs with boldness and purpose.

By the end of the 31 days, you will feel encouraged, empowered, and renewed. "Answer the Call" will leave you transformed, ready to live your faith in real, actionable ways, embodying the teachings of Scripture in every area of your life.